Are We Ready for the Ring?

Help for Couples Considering Engagement

Rob Green

New Growth Press
newgrowthpress.com

New Growth Press, Greensboro, NC 27401
newgrowthpress.com

Cover Design: David Drummond
Interior Typesetting and Ebook: Lisa Parnell, lparnellbookservices.com

ISBN: 978-1-64507-546-2 (paperback)
ISBN: 978-1-64507-547-9 (ebook)

Library of Congress Cataloging-in-Publication Data
Names: Green, Rob (Robert Eric) author
Title: Are we ready for the ring? : help for couples considering engagement / Rob Green.
Description: Greensboro, NC : New Growth Press, [2026] | Includes bibliographical references. | Audience term: Christians
Identifiers: LCCN 2026027039 (print) | LCCN 2026027040 (ebook) | ISBN 9781645075462 paperback | ISBN 9781645075479 ebook
Subjects: LCSH: Marriage—Religious aspects—Christianity | Betrothal—Religious aspects—Christianity | Marriage counseling
Classification: LCC BV835 .G7253 2026 (print) | LCC BV835 (ebook)
LC record available at https://lccn.loc.gov/2026027039
LC ebook record available at https://lccn.loc.gov/2026027040

Printed in Colombia

30 29 28 27 26   1 2 3 4 5

Contents

Introduction

Welcome to a Joy-Filled Journey

> **The Big Idea:** As you think together about whether you are ready for the ring, remember that you aren't looking for perfection from either of you; instead, you are looking to Jesus for humility, wisdom, an openness to follow his will, and a willingness to grow and change to be more like him.

ENGAGEMENTS ARE EXCITING moments. A man meets with his girlfriend's father and requests his blessing. He saves money to buy a ring that he hopes will serve as a lifelong illustration of his love for her. He thinks carefully about the engagement moment, planning every detail. Some of my friends made elaborate and even impressive engagement plans that included photographers, other family members, scavenger hunts, flowers, special food, and specific clothing. Some men and women are willing to take the leap of engagement quickly while others prefer a longer period of dating and discernment.

Even though it's fun to make your actual engagement a special memory, before that happens, you both have to decide whether this is a commitment you are ready to make. Thankfully, God has provided the Bible to give you his wisdom as you make this decision.

I'm excited and thankful that you want help in working through this decision. I am encouraged that you want to study, learn, pray, and evaluate as you answer the question, "Are we ready for the ring?"

Who Is This Book For?

If you are part of a Jesus-believing dating relationship and wondering if you are ready to move forward in your relationship toward engagement, this book is for you. Engagement is a big step! It is exciting and terrifying at the same time. So I hope this book will provide clarity for both of you as you discern the Lord's will.

If you are not part of a Jesus-believing dating relationship, this book may not be for you. But if you are reading this because you are curious to know what a Jesus follower has to say about marriage and commitment, then I am so glad you are here. We will explain the good news of Jesus Christ later in this work. It is my hope that reading this resource will result in you having a personal and saving relationship with Jesus.

If you are the parents of someone who is dating seriously, you also might be interested in reading this book. After all, it was my children's relationships that pushed me to write this resource. Our children's relationships are exciting and scary for us too. We rejoice with our children, for as Proverbs 18:22 says, "He who finds a wife finds a good thing And obtains favor from the Lord." The same can be said for our daughters who find a godly husband. However, relationships are also scary because we have seen how much pain a bad relationship can create. We know that some relationships end up in sinful oppression and evil. With all our hearts, we want to help our children avoid relationships like that. Parents, I hope this book provides some suggestions for having your own good conversations with your children about marriage and commitment. Even if your children are not interested in reading this book,

"Pastors, parents, and friends—give this to the people you love who are in a relationship. It will raise all the important conversations that too many couples never seriously consider. This book will provide wisdom for big decisions ahead."

Edward T. Welch, CCEF Faculty; author

"So many couples rush to the altar without asking the right questions or even knowing what to look for. Rob shows couples how to evaluate their spiritual trajectory without falling into the trap of perfectionism. This book provides a plan for gracious relational discernment."

Brad Bigney, Lead Pastor, Grace Fellowship Church, Florence, KY; ACBC certified counselor; author of *Gospel Treason*

"Rob Green combines his counseling experience, pastoral concerns, and fatherly passion to guide the person considering the next step beyond dating. I can't wait to recommend this insightful tool to my single friends, my counseling and pastoral students, and at some point, my grandchildren."

Robert D. Jones, Professor and Chair of Biblical Counseling and Practical Theology, The Southern Baptist Theological Seminary; author of *Pursuing Peace* and *Uprooting Anger*

"Many sincere Christians give either too little thought before becoming engaged, relying mainly on attraction and compatibility, or too much, becoming paralyzed by uncertainty while waiting for every element to perfectly align. *Are We Ready for the Ring?* wisely guides couples through questions that truly matter from God's point of view, equipping them to move forward with biblical wisdom and confidence. I gladly commend it to every prospective couple and those who disciple them."

John Henderson, Associate Professor of Biblical Counseling and Practical Theology, The Southern Baptist Theological Seminary

"What a practical book! *Are We Ready for the Ring?* wisely addresses the specific needs of dating couples. Each brief chapter is filled with insight, and I especially appreciate the big idea and reflection sections. This manual is valuable not only for the couple but also for parents, family members, mentors, singles ministry leaders, young adult ministers, and youth pastors."

Bob Kellemen, Author of *Gospel-Centered Marriage Counseling* and *Gospel-Centered Family Counseling*

"The second biggest commitment someone can make in life is marriage. But how does someone know if they've found the right person or if they are ready for that commitment? Rob Green answers those questions and many more in this excellent book. He draws on Scripture and decades of pastoral and counseling wisdom to help people discern their next steps. *Are We Ready for The Ring*? is the resource I have been waiting to share with people."

Curtis W. Solomon, Associate Professor and Program Coordinator of Biblical Counseling, Boyce College

"This book reflects Rob's biblical conviction, pastoral warmth, and practical wisdom that have marked his ministry for decades. *Are We Ready for the Ring?* is an excellent resource that will help couples pursue marriage with discernment and Christ-centered hope. We look forward to using it in our ministry with pre-engaged couples."

Kevin Carson, Pastor, Sonrise Baptist Church, Ozark, MO; executive director, Biblical Counseling Coalition

"It's so easy to see through rose-colored glasses when you're dating. But even if you want to make sure you're seeing clearly, it can be hard to figure out how to take those glasses off. *Are You Ready for the Ring?* is a helpful tool for couples who genuinely want to make wise relationship decisions. I would strongly encourage dating couples and those speaking into their lives to benefit from the wisdom Rob offers."

Amy Baker, Ministry Resource Director, Faith Church, Lafayette, IN

"Rob Green's *Tying the Knot* has helped countless couples prepare for God-honoring marriages. *Are We Ready for the Ring?* continues that legacy, offering practical biblical wisdom grounded in decades of faithful pastoral ministry. This is the book I would want my students—and my own children—to read as they prayerfully consider getting engaged."

Trent A. Rogers, Dean, School of Biblical and Theological Studies, Cedarville University

"Young adults need wisdom to prepare well for engagement. This book provides biblical instruction, realistic examples, and practical application for anyone considering engagement. I highly recommend this resource to both young adults and their mentors. Read this book, walk in the way of wisdom, and enjoy relationships God's way!"

Ross Reeder, Pastor of College and Student Ministries, Faith Church

"This brief book covers a host of issues and practical help for couples considering whether they are ready for the lifetime commitment of marriage. I love Rob's approach to pre-engagement counseling and preparation before a commitment is made. This book also provides very helpful information for those who might already be engaged as they consider a marriage that would glorify God."

Stuart Scott, Coordinator and Trainer, BCMW; member care director, ACBC you can influence them with the biblical truths and wisdom contained in it.

What Goals Do I Have for You?

My goal for you is Christlikeness. I hope that Jesus becomes so important and amazing to you that you want to love, fear, and know him more, which is part of how you grow in wisdom for this big step (Proverbs 1:7). I hope your relationship with Jesus motivates you to Christian growth, stirs in you a willingness to work spiritually, and expands your knowledge of the depths of God's love for you in Christ. My goal is not to give you a list to check off so you can get engaged. I'm sure that some couples reading this book will ultimately conclude that they need to end their current relationship and look elsewhere for a spouse. I do not consider that a failure. At the same time, other couples might grow, change, mature, and develop their relationship and decide that taking the next step toward marriage would please the Lord.

Please note—and I will say this several times through the book—the goal is not perfection. You don't need a perfect relationship to move forward. Someday, all followers of Jesus will be like him because we will see him as he is, but that is not this day (1 John 3:2). As you work through this material, it might seem that to move toward marriage everyone and everything must be perfect! But your answer to every question or issue listed in this book does not need to have a perfect score. As I wrote this book, I often thought about how my wife and I did not have a perfect score before we got married, let alone engaged.

Perfection? No. A humble attitude toward Jesus that results in growing love, fear, and knowledge? Absolutely! Through his Word, God emphasizes the sufficiency of Scripture and growth in Christlikeness. Sufficiency is important because we all must have a source of authority. God gave us his Word for many reasons, among them to share wisdom for how to live in our beautiful but twisted world. Growing to be more like Jesus is important because the Lord wants us to mature and be conformed to the image of Jesus one step at a time. We can please God but still need to please him more (1 Thessalonians 4:1, 10), love him but not understand the full dimensions of his love (Ephesians 3:14–19), or fear him but not enough to control our actions (Ecclesiastes 12:13–14).

How Preengagement Counseling Differs from Premarital Counseling

Often, those who are looking for help preengagement may read through a premarital resource. While this strategy can work for some, not all the issues raised in premarital counseling will apply to a couple who has not definitely decided to get engaged. It can also create a significant challenge during the actual premarital period. Couples may not get much value out of the premarital counseling because "they already did it before the engagement" and may not think they have more to discuss.

This tension, along with the concern for perfectionism, were the two greatest obstacles for me in preparing, teaching, and writing about this subject. While I feel the tension, there are a few things that apply to both stages. In my previous book *Tying the Knot*, I used "Jesus as the center" as part of every chapter title. I wanted Jesus to have center stage in every topic discussed. I still do! But this book does have substantial differences from a premarital resource.

- At this stage in your relationship, you are deciding whether or not you should get married. So preengagement counseling helps couples **decide** if they believe God is honored by furthering, delaying, or stopping the relationship. Any of those three outcomes could be wise and pleasing to Jesus.

- Premarital counseling, on the other hand, **prepares** couples for marriage. This means getting ready to live in a covenant relationship before the Lord, which they've already decided to do. This does not mean that an engagement can never be broken. Sometimes one learns late in the process that their relationship should not move toward marriage. But we normally expect engagements to lead to marriage.

Do You Need a Mentor to Go Through This Book with You?

You can work through this material without a mentor or counselor. However, there are several good reasons for having a mentor. First, a mentor can celebrate with you the Lord's work. This can be a significant source of joy and encouragement. Second, mentors provide accountability to finish the task. It is easy to start something, but can be hard to finish. Third, mentors encourage honesty and are more likely to spot unaddressed problems in your relationship. Fourth, when you ask someone to mentor you, you are doing them a favor. Every believer is responsible to serve (Ephesians 4:11–16), and they may find it a joy to walk alongside you. In the process, they might discover a few weaknesses in their own relationship.

Required? Of course not. Valuable and recommended? Absolutely.

A Prayer for Your Journey

Let's start this journey with the prayer requests from Ephesians 1:18–23 in mind:

> *I pray that* the eyes of your heart may be enlightened, so that you will know what is the hope of His calling, what are the riches of the glory of His inheritance in the saints, and what is the surpassing greatness of His

> power toward us who believe. *These are* in accordance with the working of the strength of His might which He brought about in Christ, when He raised Him from the dead and seated Him at His right hand in the heavenly *places*, far above all rule and authority and power and dominion, and every name that is named, not only in this age but also in the one to come. And He put all things in subjection under His feet, and gave Him as head over all things to the church, which is His body, the fullness of Him who fills all in all.

Paul prays that our hearts would be enlightened so that we understand the glorious destiny associated with his calling and that we would understand the resurrection power that works in us. We need both to live for him. Enjoy what follows, and let's see what the Lord will do.

Chapter 1
Share a Love for Jesus

The Big Idea: Engagement is an exciting step for two people who love Jesus and desire to grow both personally and as a couple to accomplish all God's plans and purposes. We will explore what it looks like when you both have embraced gospel living as your way of life.

DESIRING A CHRISTIAN marriage and wanting Christ at the center of your relationship is a wonderful place to start. But how does that happen? It's not automatic. It must begin with both of you having Jesus at the center of your life.

Some dating couples might find it surprising that my first point is not about their relationship. But this is a key truth to understand. In his book *What Did You Expect?* Paul Tripp suggests that the person you date is not the person you marry.[1] He explains that while we are dating, we present the best version of ourselves. I'm sure you can say yes to that! It is only after the wedding that the "real you" appears. In his work, *Marry Wisely, Marry Well*, Ernie Baker says that personal preparation is the first step toward making a wise marriage decision.[2] Those who help couples with struggling marriages know that when Jesus is not important to one or both members in a marriage, there can be tremendous pain, hurt, and suffering.

The Bible is crystal clear that Jesus must be our first and highest priority.

> And He said to him, "'You shall love the Lord your God with all your heart, and with all your soul, and with all your mind.' This is the great and foremost commandment. The second is like it, 'You shall love your neighbor as yourself.' On these two commandments hang the whole Law and the Prophets." (Matthew 22:37–40)

The church at Ephesus receives a shocking rebuke in Revelation 2:4: "But I have *this* against you, that you have left your first love." All of us, including both of you, are called to love the Lord with all your heart, soul, and mind.

The story of King Josiah is one of my all-time favorites (2 Kings 22:1–23:27 and 2 Chronicles 34). Josiah becomes king at eight years old when the country is a spiritual mess. His father and grandfather were wicked and led the nation astray. They rejected the Lord and served the other so-called gods of the nations around them. It seems like a recipe for disaster—an unfaithful nation and an eight-year-old king. Yet, amid all the unfaithfulness within and the dangers without, Josiah's heart is soft toward the Lord. During his rule, he destroys the places of idol worship, eliminates the unfaithful priests, reestablishes the reading of the Bible, and celebrates Passover. The Lord summarizes Josiah's life in 2 Kings 23:25 like this: "Before him there was no king like him who turned to the Lord with all his heart and with all his soul and with all his might, according to all the law of Moses; nor did any like him arise after him." May the Lord grant the same heart to you.

How do you became someone who turns to God with your whole heart? The Bible emphasizes how that begins with growing in the fear of the Lord. We all struggle with the fear of man. When we fear what people might think, say, or do to us, we can go badly wrong. By contrast, fear of the Lord—putting God first in our lives and caring more about what he thinks and wants than anyone else—is the beginning of wisdom (Proverbs 1:7, 9:10). The fear of the Lord has two sides. First, there is a worship, respect, and love for God that encourages us to do what is right. We desire to do what is right out of reverence for God. Second, we are afraid to do the things he says are wrong. I once asked a man who had committed adultery on numerous occasions with multiple women whether he feared God's discipline. He said that he knew it was wrong, but he did not believe the Lord would do anything about it. Those who do not fear the Lord have few constraints on their behavior. Proper fear of the Lord will protect you from wrong and motivate you to do right.

Paul prayed in Ephesians 1:18–23 that God's people would know the hope of his calling, the glory of his inheritance, and the surpassing greatness of his power working in us. These are more than mere words. We have hope. We know that he will work in us until the end (Philippians 1:6), that he will make us like Jesus (Romans 8:28–29), and that all his promises are yes in Jesus (2 Corinthians 1:20). This stabilizes us amid whatever turmoil we might experience. When a person believes that God's power works in us, then he or she can live with courage. When we know God's power and love, we want to live to please him in every way.

Living to please God isn't possible without knowing the gospel. The Bible says that without faith it is impossible to please God. We cannot earn our salvation or a right standing before him. We are, by nature, far from God, going our own way—this is what the Bible calls sin (Isaiah 53:6). Have you ever noticed how self-centered you are? That's natural, isn't it? And it's also the source of every wrong. We can't change ourselves (have you tried?), but Jesus can and will when you ask him. He came to earth as a man and lived every day to please God, fearing only him. Then he died, not for his sins (he had none) but for yours and mine. His resurrection was God's yes over his sacrifice for his people. Because he lives, all who turn to him and ask for forgiveness are welcomed into his kingdom to live forever with him. If you have never turned to Jesus, asked for forgiveness, and given your whole life to him, today can be that day!

> If you confess with your mouth Jesus *as* Lord, and believe in your heart that God raised Him from the dead, you will be saved; for with the heart a person believes, resulting in righteousness, and with the mouth he confesses, resulting in salvation. (Romans 10:9–10)

If you have a saving relationship with Jesus, then God fills you with his Spirit, so now you have his power to love, accept, and forgive. As you follow Jesus, you will grow more like him—speaking the truth in love, forgiving deeply, and letting grace cover your relationship.

A Christian marriage should always begin with two people who each have a strong personal relationship with the Lord. Don't be afraid to put God first! He will lead you and give you what is best. At a conference, I met a newly married couple who told me that before they met, they both wanted to be married, but they also both believed the Lord was leading them to serve him in places where potential spouses would be difficult to find. Yet, as they loved the Lord and followed him faithfully, God did what neither expected—he gave them to each other. They would never have met if they hadn't put God first.

How Can I Know?

You might agree with everything I just wrote, yet you still wonder whether it is true for you or for the one you are dating. To some degree, we can't know for certain about the spiritual commitment of our future spouse. However, I believe that the following five characteristics are true for those who love, fear, and know the Lord today and desire to grow in the future.

Characteristic #1: They openly discuss the Lord

> Oh give thanks to the LORD, for He is good, For His lovingkindness is everlasting. Let the redeemed of the LORD say *so,* Whom He has redeemed from the hand of the adversary. (Psalm 107:1–2)

Have you noticed that we talk about what's important to us? I was raised in Columbus, Ohio. When I was young, both of my parents went to school at Ohio State. On special occasions, we went to the campus location of Baskin Robbins for ice cream while one of my parents took a night class. Later, I attended and graduated from Ohio State. While I do not make Ohio State football the theme of my life, I want Ohio State to win and Michigan to lose every Saturday. It is part of my history and my life, and it's even a small piece of my joy.

By God's grace, my wife and I have three children. They bring me great joy. I love talking to and about our children. Two are married and live near us. Their lives are moving fast, and there is always something to discuss. Our youngest and only girl is moving into adulthood.

The Lord has given me an incredible ministry. At times, I have to pinch myself to see if it is a dream. Faith Church has been my home for most of my working career. I preach regularly, lead two adult Bible fellowships, counsel, teach, and lead a Master of Arts in Biblical Counseling program. It almost seems unreal.

My point is this: Family, ministry, and Ohio State are part of my life. They give me joy, and, sooner or later, these subjects find their way out of my mouth. They are part of my DNA, and they are unchanging. Ohio State will be my team until I die, regardless of where I live. My wife and children are part of who I am. Nothing could change that. Even if God called me to serve somewhere other than Faith Church, that ministry would always remain part of who I am. These are things that make me tick. You have your own set of items. Make no mistake; everyone has things important to them.

So then, what about the Lord? Can you go on ten dates and not talk about what Jesus did in saving you? Can you go on ten dates and not talk about the ways he is working in your life? We speak about the things that are important to us. Do you talk about Jesus and then watch as your boyfriend or girlfriend changes the subject? Does your boyfriend or girlfriend seem energized by the Lord? Even more central, does your boyfriend or girlfriend believe that the Lord is important? I am not suggesting that every date requires a time dedicated to Bible study and prayer, but is the Lord part of the conversation, even normal conversations? Wisdom suggests that those who do not speak about the Lord during dating will not speak much about the Lord after marriage.

Characteristic #2: They consistently have personal devotions and are engaged at church

> How can a young man keep his way pure? By keeping *it* according to Your word. With all my heart I have sought You; Do not let me wander from Your commandments. Your word I have treasured in my heart, That I may not sin against You. (Psalm 119:9–11)

Believers are taught early in their relationship with Jesus that basic spiritual disciplines are an important part of the Christian life. Reading the Bible, praying, and faithfully participating in a local church are part of the foundation for a healthy Christian life. It would be great to see you both encouraging and even leading the relationship in this way. If either of you believes you must guilt the other into Bible reading or church attendance, that is a warning sign for the relationship. These actions might be some of the first to disappear as the relationship continues to move forward.

You can also consider with what attitude you both go to church. Do you come late, leave early, and act like attending church is a burden? How each of you attends church might provide a window into your relationships with Jesus. Are you actively participating in the discipleship ministries of the church, including a small group, an adult Bible fellowship, or an equipping class?

Characteristic #3: They serve God and others

> As each one has received a *special* gift, employ it in serving one another as good stewards of the manifold grace of God. Whoever speaks, *is to do so* as one who is speaking the utterances of God; whoever serves *is to do so* as one who is serving by the strength which God supplies; so that in all things God may be glorified through Jesus Christ, to whom belongs the glory and dominion forever and ever. Amen. (1 Peter 4:10–11)

Meaningful service is part of our stewardship responsibility to the Lord. He equips and works through us so we can serve him and the church. Some parents teach their children service at an early age. However, it may be that your family or your friend's family have not had that as part of their family life or goals. Without focusing on perfection, do you both believe and practice the stewardship of one's calling from the Lord?

Since serving can be challenging, it also reveals another aspect of a person's love, fear, and knowledge of the Lord. Is the Lord worth sacrificing for? Does his finished work on the cross and ongoing ministry in our lives call forth a loving response in return? Do you want others to experience the same love, forgiveness, and grace of Jesus that you enjoy? As a father, I wanted my dating-age children to make sacrifices to serve Jesus.

I hoped that the same would be true for their future spouses. In fact, I hoped that they would serve together.

Wisdom once again reminds us that those who faithfully serve the Lord while dating are more likely to serve the Lord in their marriage.

Characteristic #4: They have a faithful track record

> We give thanks to God always for all of you, making mention of *you* in our prayers; constantly bearing in mind your work of faith and labor of love and steadfastness of hope in our Lord Jesus Christ in the presence of our God and Father, knowing, brethren beloved by God, *His* choice of you; for our gospel did not come to you in word only, but also in power and in the Holy Spirit and with full conviction; just as you know what kind of men we proved to be among you for your sake. You also became imitators of us and of the Lord, having received the word in much tribulation with the joy of the Holy Spirit, so that you became an example to all the believers in Macedonia and in Achaia. (1 Thessalonians 1:2–7)

Remember that this resource is not designed to set an expectation of perfection for either of you prior to engagement. Jesus will be at work changing us from the day of our conversion until the we meet him face to face. We are not and will not be perfect before marriage and certainly not during marriage. But, while expecting perfection is one ditch we want to avoid, another ditch is expecting nothing. God calls his people to be faithful in following Jesus, and you should be looking for that in yourself and your significant other.

Anyone can fake it for a while. Faithfulness for five minutes is not Christian faithfulness. A friend shared with me that one of his children was experiencing difficult times. His child had recently married, and the spouse turned out to be someone very different from what the family believed. My friend's child learned about an ongoing adulterous relationship and financial mismanagement, as well as experiencing abuse. It was a nightmare. Perhaps their spouse was such a skilled manipulator and deceiver that no one could have known in advance. But wisdom means we make an attempt to see the person as they genuinely are.

When Paul writes to the church at Thessalonica, he thanks them for their work of faith, labor of love, and steadfastness of hope, which was an example (1 Thessalonians 1:2–3). If perfection is not the standard, what about being an example to others?

Some enter dating relationships with life-dominating sin issues that are now in the past. Perhaps one or both of you have struggled with addictions like pornography, gambling, alcohol, drugs, or others. Consider what a faithful track record would look like for each in you in each situation. A few questions to ask might include:

- How long did the addiction last in comparison to the amount of time freed from it?
- What led to stopping the addiction (an ultimatum, biblical repentance, legal consequences)?
- What fruits of repentance can be seen? What has replaced the addiction in the person's heart?

I will say more in a later chapter about how to address these matters if they are active struggles, but for now, I want to encourage you both to look for a person who is seeking a lifestyle of faith and who is growing in repentance. There isn't a Bible passage that explains the exact amount of time this might take. However, the testimony of Scripture is clear: We are prone to wander. Even the great reforms of Kings Hezekiah and Josiah were short-lived. Maybe if our standard is being an example to others, like the Thessalonians were, it might save a lot of heartache.

Characteristic #5: They have a humble heart about change

> But He gives a greater grace. Therefore *it* says, "GOD IS OPPOSED TO THE PROUD, BUT GIVES GRACE TO THE HUMBLE." (James 4:6)

Those who love, fear, and know the Lord are sensitive to the ways he wants them to change. Rather than act as if they are always doing the right thing, they are bothered by their own sin. When they speak with unbiblical words, they acknowledge it and want to change. When they express sinful anger, they regret it and the way it impacted those who felt it.

Through your dating relationship, you should see change. Both of you should be willing to ask for forgiveness—and to hear the other tell them their concerns. Each of you should be growing in sensitivity to each other. It's true that we cannot change others. Future spouses are encouraged not to think that they will bring about change in the other person. But you should both be able to see the ways that the Lord is changing you.

Some people give lipservice for change but do not want to experience the pain associated with real change. The root of this is pride and an unwillingness to admit that they are a sinner saved by grace. If either of you consistently acts like this, then whatever immaturity and rebellion exist will remain into the engagement and marriage.

It is not enough to acknowledge the need for change with words. Red flags in a relationship include defensiveness when issues are raised, an inability to say "I'm sorry," and acting as if they didn't do anything wrong when challenged. Look for a lifestyle of repentance and faith—where you both ask God for forgiveness and depend on Jesus's sacrifice to be washed clean. A life of faith will result in observable changes. Becoming a Christian means we ask for forgiveness for our many sins, and being faithful as a Christian means we continue to ask for forgiveness every day. Living like this will result in growing to be more like Jesus. Look for that in yourself and the one you are dating—not perfection, but growth.

I realize that this is not easy. One time I asked my wife a simple question: "Do you know why I am ten pounds heavier than I should be and can't seem to shed those pounds?" Ready for her answer? She said, "Because you eat too much." She was right. I am unwilling to experience the hunger associated with losing ten pounds. When it comes to my weight, I feel like I'm good enough, even though I readily admit that being ten pounds lighter would be good for several reasons. It is one thing to pursue marriage with a person who knows they need to grow and is actively growing, and it's something far different to pursue marriage with a person who believes and lives as though they've grown enough.

What's Your Trajectory?

Engagement is a big step. Before you shop for a ring, consider where you both are spiritually. Are you and the person you are dating people whose choices reflect that you both love, fear, and know the Lord? Do you both have reason to believe that you will continue to grow in the Lord? Since life is all about direction, consider your direction and consider the direction of your boyfriend or girlfriend. Do you both know that you have been forgiven much and that you need to depend on the Spirit every moment of every day for the grace to love God and others? Remember that the Spirit of God can change your direction at any time—all you have to do is ask for forgiveness and the grace to become more like Jesus. He is waiting to hear from you.

Reflection Questions

1. On a scale of 1–10, rate your relationship with Jesus based on the five characteristics listed above. Provide specific examples of why you are giving yourself that number.
2. On a scale of 1–10, rate your boyfriend/girlfriend's relationship with Jesus. Provide specific evidence to justify your rating.
3. What changes in either of your lives might increase these ratings and indicate a deeper walk with Jesus? Possible ideas could include:
   - Regular study of the Word
   - Talking to the Lord about your challenges, asking for strength in your weakness, and confessing your rebellion
   - Asking a spiritual leader to help you
   - Reading material such as *The Gospel Primer for Christians*[3] or *Gentle and Lowly*[4] to encourage you with gospel truth. This change to be more Christ-centered in your relationship could then be reflected with a practice: dedicating one date a month to serving your local church in some capacity, spending a portion of each date talking about what the Lord is doing in our life, or taking time once a month to discuss areas of needed spiritual growth.
4. Consider memorizing a passage of Scripture to grow in your love, fear, and knowledge of Jesus. Possible options include Matthew 11:28–30; John 10:11–18, 25–30; Romans 8:31–39; or Ephesians 2:1–10. Other Old Testament references to the Lord include Psalm 34, 42, 117; Isaiah 53.

Chapter 2
Grow in Commitment to Each Other

> **The Big Idea:** A growing relationship that is moving toward engagement should be enjoyable. Spending time together should be exciting and desirable.

"I must arise now and go about the city;
In the streets and in the squares
I must seek him whom my soul loves."
(SONG OF SOLOMON 3:2)

ARE BOTH YOU and your significant other committed to your relationship? You can't be engaged on your own! So you both need to be on the same page. Let me illustrate this by telling a personal story. Before I dated my wife, I met a girl at college that I thought was wonderful. She was a faithful follower of Jesus. She was fun to be around and easy on the eyes. I tried to win her. She was not interested. In my mind, she needed to move me from the friend zone to the possible husband category. In her mind, I needed to leave her alone. While this initially stung, she was doing the right thing.

While I am sure she could identify many of my character flaws and weaknesses, at the end of the day, she simply did not want me. I do not see that as sinful or mean. She could not imagine a life with me. Rather than pretend like she could, she refused to give me any hope that she would change her mind. It was a hard reality to accept, but in hindsight, I can see that she was caring for me by being honest about her feelings.

A friend shared with me that she once dated a man for thirty minutes. She said yes to his initial request and within the hour decided it had to end. Both my friend and her ex-boyfriend (for thirty minutes!) are now happily married to other people. When I asked why the relationship ended so quickly, she said that there was nothing "wrong" with him; he loved the Lord, served faithfully, and was kind and caring. She simply could not imagine life with him.

I invited a girl to join me in a romantic exploration and a boy had made a similar offer to one of my friends. In both of these cases, one person said no. They were not interested in going on that adventure. So here is my question for you: Do you want to move to engagement thinking that you are ready to spend your life with this person? Should you marry, you will invest more into that person than anyone else in your life. You will serve them more than anyone else. They will be a source of joy and pain. Are you sure you are ready for the next level of commitment?

Jacob and Rachel's Story

Jacob and Rachel's story in Genesis has many turns, not all of which honor the Lord, but they do form a love story. After stealing his brother Esau's inheritance, Jacob must flee his father's home, and his mother sends him to his Uncle Laban's home where he meets Rachel.

When they meet, Jacob is awestruck by Rachel's beauty. The Bible says that Rachel is beautiful of form and face (Genesis 29:17). Jacob could not have hoped for anything better. He has successfully journeyed to his planned destination, he still has his father's blessing and birthright, and Laban welcomes him into the family home and offers to give Rachel's hand in marriage to Jacob in return for labor. Jacob loves Rachel and has Laban's commitment to give her to him (Genesis 29:19). How could it get any better for Jacob? Genesis 29:20 says, "So Jacob served seven years for Rachel and they seemed to him but a few days because of his love for her." We know that the rest of the story is chaotic. However, Genesis 29:20 serves as a benchmark to describe one person's view of another.

Commitment Tests

What follows are two application tests for how committed you are to your boyfriend or girlfriend.

Willingness to Sacrifice

I first heard as a child that a man will do anything for the woman he loves. That sounded like garbage to my young ears. So the first time I heard about Jacob working for seven years for a woman, I could not believe it. She might have been beautiful, but seven years? As a math guy, I started doing the calculations, and it never added up. Things changed when I met my wife. We started dating, and the more I got to know her, the better I understood Jacob.

While we dated, she continued pursuing the goals she believed the Lord had for her. She left Columbus, Ohio, to attend a Bible college in Pennsylvania to train for medical missions. The school was five hundred miles away from where I lived. I didn't think it would be a big deal. I was wrong; being apart from her practically killed me. I bought phone cards so I could speak with her (for the younger generation, there were no cell phones, and long distance calling was billed separately). Our calls had to be arranged because in her dorm there was only one phone per floor, and all the girls had to share it (I realize this must sound like we were born before the civilized world).

One week I decided I just had to see her. On Friday I went to my classes. My Digital Logic and Design class ended at 3 p.m. As soon as class ended, I ran to my car and began the five-hundred-mile journey (in the days of a fifty-five miles per hour speed limit!). I arrived at where I was staying for the night around midnight. We spent Saturday together, but a campus speed bump ripped the muffler off my car and split one of the exhaust pipes. An empty soup can, tin snips, zip ties, and a couple coat hangers later, I started my five-hundred-mile trip back home after church on Sunday.

The first time my boys heard that story, they thought I was crazy. I told them that they couldn't understand because they hadn't yet met the person they did not want to live without. When you meet that person, it is no longer crazy. Jacob working seven years for Rachel finally made sense to me. The sacrifices are worth it. The long drives, phone card expenses, letters, and personal investment was all worth it. Ironically, I have seen both my sons do similar things. One found time to make special trips to Iowa for his wife. The other drove six hundred miles on a Friday after work to surprise his girlfriend at her home. Suddenly, what seemed completely insane was nothing—in the way that seven years was but a few days to Jacob because of his love for Rachel.

I tell my stories from a man's perspective. However, my wife and my sons' girlfriends made sacrifices too. They have invested time, money, and energy to make us feel special, cared for, and loved. They too have taken the initiative to plan and organize blessings for us.

Your commitment to each other is part of being ready for a ring. Commitment is seen in the sacrifices you are both willing to make for each other. What are your seven years' wages? What are your five-hundred-mile drives? What sacrifices show your investment in this relationship? Jesus says in Matthew 6:21, "Where your treasure is, there your heart will be also."

Excitement in Being Together

I have long been interested in the best way to interpret the Song of Solomon. Some believe it is figurative for the love Jesus has for the church—his bride—while others believe it describes a real human relationship. Once you agree with the latter, as I do, then the question is whether the book presents a progression of the relationship or a collection of seven songs celebrating marital love. Again, I believe the latter is correct. That opens yet another question: Is Solomon describing his relationship to his favorite wife (remember he had seven hundred wives and three hundred concubines according to 1 Kings 11:3) or is this what would have happened if he had followed the Lord's plan for marriage between one man and one woman? Again, I believe the latter is correct.

Taking this view of the Song of Solomon helps us think about relationships. Do people get married because they feel trapped, or like somehow they will disappoint their parents or other loved ones unless they go through with marriage? I think one lesson we can learn from the Song of Solomon is excitement. All through the Song, the two long to be together. When apart, they even solicit the help of others to find their loved one. Although this book is about preparing for engagement and not the marital love of the Song of Solomon, I still believe that excitement plays an important role.

A friend of mine once struggled with his son's broken engagement. They were just a few weeks from the wedding. They had taken his fiancée on family vacations, treated her as part of the family, and staged most of the wedding decorations at their home, waiting for the upcoming big day. He could not believe it was over and asked me for help in thinking through the whole situation.

After affirming his pain and loss, I offered two suggestions. First, lead each family member to grieve this loss. A broken engagement so close to the wedding day is devastating to everyone. Allow each family member to lament to the Lord, reaffirm their trust in God, and commit to living under his sovereignty. Ensure that there is a lot of grace in your family relationships. Each person needs to heal, and not everyone will be on the same timeline.

Second, celebrate. Take your family out for a party. This suggestion caught him off guard initially. It sounded strange, even harsh. However, as we spoke, he understood. I asked him to remember his wedding day. Was he excited? Did he believe he found the person who would rejoice with him over all their blessings and grieve with him over their losses? As he looked back, could he see that his wife was a joy to his heart all these years? He happily agreed.

Then I asked, "Do you want the same thing for your son?" Now a party made sense. Of course, he wanted his son to marry a woman who wanted to be there with his son through all the ups and downs the Lord had planned. He wanted his son to enjoy the amazing blessings of living his whole life with one woman who was nuts about him. Grieve, yes. There was real loss. But there was another sense in which they had all avoided a disaster. For that, it is time to celebrate.

Sometimes dating relationships end because you realize that you do not want to spend your lives together. While ending the relationship may create grief in the short term, it is much better to allow your boyfriend or girlfriend to find a person who wants to share life with them. It is also much better for you.

What's Your Trajectory?

Engagement is a big step. Before you shop for a ring, consider whether you are excited to spend your life together. Have you and your boyfriend or girlfriend sacrificed to be with each other? Is there a clear desire from you both to be together? Relationships should not be forced. If your dating is not producing joy, then maybe the most God-honoring next step is to end it. That will give each of you permission to grieve and to begin preparing for what the Lord has for each of you. On the other hand, maybe this is a time to journal your thoughts and take them to the Lord. The Lord desires that we cast our cares on him as an expression of our humility toward him (1 Peter 5:6–7). You might find that, as you pray, the Lord confirms to both of you that ring shopping is in your near future.

Reflection Questions

1. Provide three specific examples of how both of you have already sacrificed for the other.
2. Identify two sacrifices you could make that would clearly communicate to your boyfriend or girlfriend that you are ready for the next stage of commitment.
3. Write a paragraph about how you managed any times of separation (internship, summer break, etc.) and your attitude about that separation.

Chapter 3
Be United in Purpose, Convictions, and Direction

The Big Idea: Joyful, God-honoring marriages are characterized by unity about what matters most. During this stage of your relationship, you can speak openly about the purpose you believe the Lord has for you, your core convictions, and the direction of your life. Agreement in these areas will create growing unity that will allow you to accomplish much for Christ together.

Beyond all these things put on love,
which is the perfect bond of unity.
(COLOSSIANS 3:14)

MARRIAGE IS A wonderful journey. My wife and I have now been married thirty-two years. It's amazing to look back and see how the Lord directed our steps, and it's been a joy to live with Stephanie. That does not mean every step was easy—not at all. But our common purpose, convictions, and direction served to unify us through the journey. We might discuss how to respond to a child, whether to change the carpet, or how much to spend on a vacation, but we have never had to debate our purpose, convictions, or direction. This unity has been a foundation for our marriage. You will be ready for a ring when you have unity about the foundation of life.

It is impossible to know in advance all that the Lord might allow you to experience. Few get married thinking that infertility might be an issue, that they might experience sickness, or that they might care for a child with special needs. Few expect work challenges or outside pressures like war, a recession, or bankruptcy at the company employing them. It is a grace from God that we do not know the future challenges in advance. Those who have built their lives on the Lord and each other can respond with faith by supporting each other in the moves and shifts of life. They can navigate the valleys and mountaintops in a way that honors Jesus and continues to build their relationship.

Agreement in marriage is more difficult for those who do not share this unity. Challenges and suffering gain a faster foothold and can open a chasm. This chapter is an opportunity to assess your relationship and to take an honest look at what you are building your life on. Remember that deciding to become engaged (and living in a marriage) is not about perfection. We cannot know all that the Lord will allow in our lives. Once we decide to marry, we choose by default to walk together through whatever we experience. We pledge for richer or poorer, in sickness and in health, until death parts us. We choose to walk in unity on the day of our marriage.

Walk in Unity

It may help you to consider three areas that warrant wise and careful thought before you agree to walk together in unity.

Unity in Purpose

> But you are A CHOSEN RACE, A royal PRIESTHOOD, A HOLY NATION, A PEOPLE FOR *GOD'S* OWN POSSESSION,

> so that you may proclaim the excellencies of Him who has called you out of darkness into His marvelous light. (1 Peter 2:9)

> Therefore we also have as our ambition, whether at home or absent, to be pleasing to Him. (2 Corinthians 5:9)

In the Old Testament, the Lord chose the nation of Israel to set his affections on them. In 1 Peter, the Lord applies that same grace to all who trust in Jesus, giving us four descriptions which are full of meaning. By grace alone, Christians receive the freedom of coming into God's presence. "Holy" describes being set apart. Christians are now set apart by God and called as a people for God's own possession. We are his inheritance. Considering all the amazing grace flowing from almighty God to us, "so that" provides the appropriate response—we must proclaim his excellencies. What a privilege this purpose is!

Paul wrote to the church at Corinth to encourage them to live lives pleasing to the Lord no matter what happens. "Home" here means being in heaven and "absent" refers to his current life on earth. The Lord met him, opened his eyes to God's love in Christ, freed him from sin and death, and then led him on a journey of sharing his faith all over the world. On that journey, he saw God save all kinds of people. But Paul was also persecuted for his faith, imprisoned, and ultimately executed. Through it all, Paul's aim was simple—to please Jesus.

Do you both have these goals? Can you look at yourself and point to the ways you are aiming to proclaim Christ's greatness and please him? How about your boyfriend or girlfriend? Are you both using your gifts, abilities, and financial resources for these purposes? If the way you each use your time, gifts, and resources reveals that you're living for anything other than

Jesus (such as fun, thrills, comfort, or ease), then you must consider your options.

Deciding to get married before you are sure of your or your significant other's purpose would not be wise. Asking her to marry you or agreeing to marry him will not automatically change his or her core purposes in life. Don't believe the lie that you can change the other person. Your boyfriend's or girlfriend's actions should show that they live to proclaim the Lord's excellencies and they want to please the Lord because of their love for him. Of course, neither of you will always live only to please God. But our direction counts. In what direction are you both going—toward Jesus or toward something else?

Unity in Theological Convictions

The word "theology" means the study of God. Practically speaking, our theology is the belief system that guides our behavior. We live out what we truly believe. There are few beliefs more important than the gospel itself. What is the good news? How is a person saved from God's judgment, which their sins deserve? When Paul wrote to the Galatian churches, he knew what he had taught them, but he had heard that other teachers taught that a believer needed to obey the Mosaic Law to be a genuine Christian. Paul believed that the Galatian believers were in danger. Galatians is his only book that starts with a warning instead of a thanksgiving (Galatians 1:6–12). He calls the Galatians "foolish" because they accepted the arguments of the false teachers (Galatians 3:1, 3). He says that there is no such thing as another gospel, and those who get it wrong are accursed. Rarely do we find such intense language for so much of a letter. Yet, for Paul, the gospel message was in the balance, and therefore so was the spiritual condition of the Galatian believers.

Paul is willing to have disagreements, as he does with the church at Corinth. He is willing to exhort others who are doing reasonably well to excel still more, as he does with the church at Thessalonica. However, there are some convictions where compromise is unacceptable. There is a difference between being wrong and being wrong about the gospel. Thus, do you both have the same conviction regarding the good news of Jesus Christ? At first, that might sound like an easy question. However, let me illustrate why this subject might need to be carefully discussed.

A young man comes from a conservative Baptist background where he learns about the Baptist distinctives. He meets a young women from a traditional Church of Christ denomination. At first, they are interested because they view each other as attractive both outside and inside. They enjoy being together, and it seems like their relationship should move forward.

But as their relationship develops, they realize that they talk about salvation differently. One speaks in the language of the five *solas*, combining them into the statement, "Salvation is by grace alone through faith alone in Christ alone based on Scripture alone to the glory of God alone." The other talks about faith in Jesus and baptism. The more they talk, the more they have difficulty discerning the truth about salvation. Then they realize that it will be very difficult to raise their children in a Christian home if they cannot even explain what it means to be saved.

We do not always come from the same church backgrounds or have the same core beliefs. Couples holding different positions often, in the name of peace, move toward the least common denominator. They ask, "What beliefs can we make unimportant for the purpose of the relationship?" I understand the dilemma. Couples are trying to decide whether to move forward, and ending the relationship is painful. You might think it's better to adjust your beliefs for the sake of the relationship. This is a risky proposition, and one that needs careful thought. In some situations, the differences are minor and will not affect how you do life or serve the Lord. In other cases, they become major sources of contention.

Both of you will grow as you learn, read, study, and live out your faith. But you will find it incredibly difficult if you marry a person who does not share your same core convictions. If you cannot agree on who God is, how you are saved, what it means to grow and mature spiritually, and what kind of church you will attend, then you must have a serious conversation. The default will be to compromise, to attempt to find the least common denominator, and to avoid hard theology discussions. Don't avoid those conversations! Talking about the gospel and its core truths together will grow and strengthen both of you.

Unity in Life Direction

> Therefore be careful how you walk, not as unwise men but as wise, making the most of your time, because the days are evil. So then do not be foolish, but understand what the will of the Lord is. (Ephesians 5:15–17)

In these verses, Paul is calling us all to make wise decisions based on the will of the Lord for each of us. When it comes to life direction, we are all called to walk with Jesus, but the specifics of what we are called to do differ from one person to the next. As you decide if you are ready for the ring, it's important to make sure that you and your boyfriend or girlfriend are being called in the same direction. Having this conversation now will help both of you discern whether God is calling you to walk together as you follow Jesus.

When my wife and I were dating, I had a delightful relationship with her parents. Every Friday night was their family pizza night. When Stephanie went to Pennsylvania for school, I decided to spend each Friday evening with her parents. Our time together allowed us all to develop a deeper relationship with each other. Her parents grew to know and trust me. When

I spoke to my wife's father about marrying her, he wanted to know just one thing—whether I was planning to serve in vocational ministry. At the time, I was a senior studying engineering physics. But her father knew that she believed the Lord wanted her involved in ministry. She went to Pennsylvania for medical missions training. He wisely knew that his daughter would struggle if I was going to work as an engineer my entire life. He had no trouble or concerns about my character, my relationship with the Lord, or my theology. With those issues satisfied in his mind, his permission centered around common life direction. He knew that his daughter would only be happy if she were involved in vocational ministry because that is what she believed God was calling her to.

Another example involves one of our sons. He was spending intentional time with a girl who was committed to Jesus and interested in him. The early signs pointed to a potentially positive relationship, and as they considered starting to officially date, they decided to discuss life direction.

She was a linguist and wanted to be involved in Bible translation work. He wanted to serve Jesus but did not believe the Lord had called him to vocational ministry. He thought it might be possible to live in the States and do nonvocational ministry while she could still meaningfully participate in translation work. She, however, envisioned her life differently. She longed to live among an unreached people group, learn their language, maybe even invent writing to go with their spoken language, and then translate the Scriptures into this new written language.

Since most of the major language groups have had Scripture translated into their language, that meant she would have to live either in a jungle in South America, in a desert in Africa, or in the frozen tundra of Alaska or Canada. None of that sounded remotely appealing or even appropriate for the Lord's work in my son's life. They had no choice. By God's grace, the relationship ended before it ever got serious. This conversation, while it was painful, was also helpful and freed each of them to pursue the Lord's will for their lives. At the same time, it gave each of them the opportunity to look for someone else who would be willing to pursue the Lord in the same direction.

It's Okay to Remain Single

As you have these conversations, you might find that one of you does not feel called to be married. This is also a great choice. Many people live productive, God-honoring lives as single persons. Those who are single pastor churches, serve as vocational missionaries, lead ministries, write helpful resources, and do many other wonderful things. So even if you are dating, remember that it is not a predetermined commitment to marriage. Some singles date and then realize that the Lord is calling them to serve him as a single. Ending a relationship can be a possible positive outcome of going through this material.

What's Your Trajectory?

You might have noticed that all of the issues raised in this chapter can be resolved as you and your significant other take the time to talk with each other and communicate what you are hoping, believing, thinking, and planning for the future. These kind of deep conversations should be a growing part of your relationship. They can be a wonderful opportunity to express what you believe about God, about Jesus and his gospel, and about what he is calling you to do in your life and possibly together. And if you are not on the same page, you can ask the Spirit to help you either grow together or decide to move forward separately. Remember that Jesus is with you as you have these conversations. He will help and guide you. You might find, however, that the more you speak, the more it is obvious that you should start saving for the ring.

The longer a relationship lasts, the more invested both people are and the harder it is to end it. Having these conversations now before you move forward to engagement will help you ensure that your relationship has the solid foundation it needs for all that the Lord may bring in the future.

Reflection Questions

1. Read again the passages given in the chapter and memorize the one that resonates with you the most. Share with your significant other why you chose that passage.
2. Create a list of questions for each of the three categories to ask your boyfriend or girlfriend. Here are a few sample questions to get you started:
   - What do you believe is your ultimate purpose? How do you believe the Lord wants you to fulfill that purpose? (Purpose)
   - What are some of the hopes or dreams you have for the future? (Direction)
   - If you were to die today and the Lord should ask, "Why should I let you into my heaven?" what would you say? (Gospel/Theology)
   - Tell me about one time you shared the gospel with another person. What did you tell them that they needed to do to be saved? (Gospel)
   - If we were to get married, what would you like to be true of us five years from now? (Direction/Purpose)
3. After you have completed your list, please discuss the items with your boyfriend or girlfriend. What did this discussion teach you about your commitment to Jesus, your theological beliefs, and the ways the Lord wants you to please him?

Chapter 4

Take the Time to Really Know Each Other

The Big Idea: Dating couples arrange to spend time together when it is convenient for both of them. Married couples are together when it is convenient and inconvenient, and even when they prefer to be alone. Wisdom encourages you to understand your boyfriend or girlfriend to help you prepare for the marriage experience.

Teach me good discernment and knowledge,
For I believe in Your commandments.
(PSALM 119:66)

Two are better than one because they have
a good return for their labor.
(ECCLESIASTES 4:9)

I KNOW COUPLES that met, got engaged, and married in no time. They have gone on to have successful and long-lasting marriages. However, I have also seen quick or no dating, short engagements, and then difficult marriages. Early warning signs were ignored. The pain, hurt, and challenge is real.

In Paul Tripp's book *What Did You Expect?*, he highlights that our expectation about married life prior to marriage is different than our experience in marriage. Some of these surprises are unavoidable—marriage is very different from singleness, and in this chapter we will start by identifying some of those differences. But we are also going to discuss ways you can wisely get to know each other so that your expectations for what it is like to be married are more realistic and the surprises you encounter after marriage will be mostly pleasant ones.

Important Differences Between Dating and Marriage

A Christian marriage is a unique relationship that is patterned after Christ's relationship with his church (Ephesians 5:31–32). That mystery, which is made clear in the New Testament, could not have been predicted in advance. There was no way to know that when God gave marriage to Adam and Eve, its intimate companionship and fruitfulness could be related to Jesus and his bride. That mystery required the fullness of time for Christ's first coming.

So there are some aspects of a Christian marriage that you cannot experience during the dating or engagement periods. A Christian marriage means living together and joining together sexually, neither of which should be part of the dating relationship. Should a Christian couple choose this route, they often feel guilty about what they are doing. They know that this is not God's way to begin a married life. Some couples argue that living together mitigates the risk of marrying the wrong person, but I suggest that it increases the risk. When you live together without the commitment of marriage, people can still be on their best behavior until the wedding day. What actually occurs when couples live together is often greater practice in being inauthentic and ignoring sin against God, and it sets you up for an unpleasant surprise when things go poorly. I have seen many relationships collapse under the weight of the new lifelong commitment of marriage, despite the couple having lived together first.

As you are dating, be careful to not act as if you are married without actually being married. It is not hard to see how someone having a marriage covenant mindset too early could be deceived, harmed, and manipulated. Dating does not obligate people in the same way that marriage does. For example, Christian marriages involve leadership and submission but also teamwork. Thus, there is no "your money" or "my house." All possessions are shared and equally owned. But that is not true when you are dating.

When my wife and I were dating, she visited an amusement park where she could bungee jump for five dollars. I was not happy. I thought bungee jumping was dangerous conceptually, and the cost made me question the safety equipment! Five dollars to tie yourself to a cord and jump off a fifty-foot platform? But here is the reality: Whether she went bungee jumping or spent five dollars on it was none of my business. Stephanie could make it my business if she wanted, but she was under no obligation to consider my desires or to even tell me about it.

Prior to marriage, each person's finances are their own, including their income, debts, and savings. They earn, spend, and save as they see fit. Dating couples inform, offer advice, and discuss possible future actions, but each person makes their plans separately. It's not wise to blend your finances before you have made a marriage commitment. Too many men and women have paid off their partner's debts, purchased expensive items, or given away serious money only to later learn the whole thing was a scam. In marriage, however, we pool our resources together, agree on a plan, and then follow that plan together. Dating is characterized by freedom with money while Christian marriage is characterized by union, unity, and working together.

When you are dating, how each of you spends your time is also your own business. If you want to visit family, have a girls' or a guys' night, get extra sleep, or accomplish something for work or school, then you are free to make that decision. Of course, you will want to spend time together if you are dating, but it is one thing to do so voluntarily and another to be coerced or manipulated to spend your time the way your significant other wants you to. When you are married, time works differently. My time is not solely focused on what I want to do. Instead, I allocate my time in cooperation with Stephanie's desires. That might mean running an errand, helping a child with homework, doing something around the house, or spending time with her.

It is both unwise and risky to voluntarily give up your freedom before you both vow before God and your community that you intend to faithfully follow God's plan for marriage. But it is important to understand that when you get married, you are voluntarily giving up the freedom you have as a single person. It can take couples by surprise when they don't understand how marriage changes your choices about what you do, when you do it, and how much money you spend.

Spending Time Together

Some couples spend a surprisingly small amount of time together prior to their wedding. Many of us know a friend or family member who can share a powerful testimony of how it was love at first sight, they got married two weeks later, and now they have enjoyed sixty wonderful years together.

Praise the Lord for these stories. However, they are not the norm. And getting married without spending intentional time together often results in marriages that are neither happy nor healthy. Sometimes distance, timing, or other issues create a barrier to spending time together. On occasion, there is not much you can do about it. I do not believe it is sinful to move forward, but this chapter is about wisdom. What makes good sense? The more you allow these challenges—as significant as they are—to keep you from spending significant time together, the more risk you take that your expectations about marriage will be far from your reality.

For those who want to investigate more closely and attempt to ensure that Ecclesiastes 4:9 will be true for the two of them ("Two are better than one because they have a good return for their labor"), here are three things to look for.

Do everyday activities together

> He who walks in integrity walks securely, But he who perverts his ways will be found out. (Proverbs 10:9)

Although married couples still date after their vows, their marriage is not just about having dinner at a restaurant, going to a movie, or enjoying a favorite activity. Marriage is made up of daily stuff like work, laundry, home maintenance, communication about plans and schedules, friendships, grocery shopping, cooking, and the like. Anyone can behave for a short period. Character is revealed over time.

So it would be wise to spend time with your boyfriend or girlfriend when it is not a "date." This gives you both the opportunity to find out what the other is really like. What kind of work ethic do they have? What jokes do they share or listen to? How do they respond when something does not come easily? Perhaps instead of eating out, you could make a meal together. If the meal did not turn out perfectly, what was the reaction? What is your boyfriend or girlfriend like when they visit family? Do they put their dishes away after eating? Do they help clean up? Are they a consumer waiting for others to do for them, or are they a servant looking out for others?

Proverbs 10:9 says that people who walk in integrity walk securely. They have nothing to fear because their character speaks for itself. They are reliable because they have personal integrity. They live for Jesus regardless of what happens around them. When the day is great, they live with integrity. When the day is difficult, they live with integrity. Deceptive people are eventually found out. But all too often, that happens after the ceremony. Now is the time to do normal stuff and see what happens.

None of this is a 100 percent guarantee that you will know exactly what you are getting should you marry, but doing everyday activities together reveals character traits that would have been difficult to discover when you only spend official date time together.

Observe them under pressure

For years I struggled to understand God's words to Job in chapters 38–42 after reading Job 1:22, which says, "Through all this Job did not sin nor did he blame God," and Job 2:10, which recounts Job's words to his wife: "But he said to her, 'You speak as one of the foolish women speaks. Shall we indeed accept good from God and not accept adversity?' In all this Job did not sin with his lips." Job's wife encouraged him to curse God and die. Amid Job's intense suffering, including his wife tempting him to curse God, Job remains blameless. Job's friends see his pain and choose to quietly remain for seven days, mourning his pain with him (sadly, when they did speak, they weren't particularly helpful). Yet by chapter 38, the Lord corrects Job. What happened?

Job's friends believe that Job has sinned against the Lord and refuses to acknowledge it. They believe that the calamity against Job is God's discipline. They advise him to repent, but Job does not need to repent, as 1:22 and 2:10 make clear. Job willingly accepts God's plans as part of his sovereignty, instead of repenting. Job's friends, in turn, only see stubbornness and self-righteousness. They double down on Job, confronting him more aggressively throughout the book. Job then defends himself more aggressively. This cycle runs for thirty-six chapters before God breaks through their arguing to correct all of them.

The Lord has strong words for Job's friends (Job 42:7–9) because they are wrong about Job. However, the constant pressure of Job's suffering and the three friends who blast Job also result in a pride and self-righteousness in him. As the Lord corrects him, Job agrees that he needs to stop talking and asks the Lord to teach and forgive him (Job 40:3–5; 42:1–6). Job needed to be humbled.

Job's story has implications for you. First, how does your boyfriend or girlfriend respond to pressure? Even Job struggled under the weight of suffering and his friends' accusations. However, when confronted by the Lord, he humbles himself. He admits that he needs to listen rather than speak and request forgiveness rather than justify himself. Is that what you do under pressure? How about your significant other?

Second, Paul teaches that our tribulations (i.e., pressure) produce proven character.

> And not only this, but we also exult in our tribulations, knowing that tribulation brings about perseverance; and perseverance, proven character; and proven character, hope; and hope does not disappoint, because the love of God has been poured out within our hearts through the Holy Spirit who was given to us. (Romans 5:3–5)

I remember hearing Paul Tripp give an illustration of this. He held an open water bottle, shook it, and then asked, "Why did water spill?" Many of us gave the answer, "Because you shook it." There is a sense in which that is true. But he then changed the question, emphasizing the word "water." Then we all understood. Water spilled because water was in the bottle. When you are dating and doing fun activities, you are not seeing the full picture. Pressure is what produces proven character, not dates to your favorite restaurant. Far too many people excuse bad moments under pressure, assuming that their true character is better. These folks have it backward. We grow more like Christ under pressure. Job sinned, but when confronted, he was quick to listen and repent. This kind of response builds proven character and hope.

What does your boyfriend or girlfriend do under pressure? Do they blameshift? Is it the professor's fault, the boss's fault, the parent's fault, or your fault? Peter reminds us that pressure is like a refiner's fire (1 Peter 1:6–7). Peter commends his audience because they endured and showed that their faith was real. Sadly, pressure sometimes reveals that your boyfriend or girlfriend is selfish and unwilling to allow it to mold and shape them to be more like Jesus. Those who respond with the humility of Job show that they are soft and sensitive to the Lord's work.

In Romans 5:1–3, Paul tells us how knowing our identity in Christ helps us rejoice in our sufferings (v. 3). We have peace with God through Christ (v. 1). We stand in grace (v. 2). And we exult in the hope of God's glory (v. 2). All three statements reflect how a person views themself. Understanding these concepts helps us have joy in tribulation, not because of the suffering, but because the end result is growing more like Christ. When you see your boyfriend or girlfriend able to remind themselves that they have peace with God, they stand in grace, and they exult in the hope of God's glory as they experience hardship, it shows you that they have the right foundation for becoming more like Jesus (Romans 8:28–29). This allows you to be a helper and supporter after marriage, and this is a major green light to move forward. Those who do not find their identity and motivation in Christ will find their identity in something else. They might even choose to find their identity in you. In that case, they will depend on you for their purpose and motivation in tribulation. But you are not equipped for that responsibility, and you will ultimately disappoint them.

Serve together

When we discussed this subject in chapter 1, the primary emphasis was on each individual's commitment to the Lord. But serving the Lord also reveals one's true character. Some ministry assignments are difficult. Caring for little children who want their parents can be a test of patience. Cleaning bathrooms tests whether a person believes they are too good or important for such a task. Weekly service tests commitment. Following the instructions of other leaders tests pride. There is a lot you can learn about each other by serving together. The way your boyfriend or girlfriend responds to others provides a clue into how they will treat you in the future.

Those who are trying to manipulate you into thinking that they are spiritual will give clues during or after the service. Here are some common red flags to pay attention to:

- Complaining about the leaders and acting as if they could do better
- Complaining about the difficulty of the assignment
- Acting as if they hate being there
- Attempting to convince you not to serve or to break a commitment
- Demanding that when they serve, you must always be at their side

If you notice any of these red flags, raise the subject with your boyfriend or girlfriend. You will learn a lot by the way they respond. Are they defensive? Do they try to make excuses and blame others (including you)? Or do they repent like Job, asking God and you for forgiveness?

Again, I am not trying to set a standard of perfection. I want couples, parents, and mentors reading this book to be gracious, compassionate, and loving toward others, not expecting a boyfriend or girlfriend to be amazing at every level. But there are times that grace, compassion, and believing the best are not virtues because they are not based on truth or facts. Don't be self-righteous and judgmental, but also make sure you don't ignore things you should care about because God cares about them.

What's Your Trajectory?

It is not wise to rush into marriage. That is especially true in our age of dating apps and websites. People can create profiles that, at their best, put their best foot forward and, at their worst, are nothing like them. When they sell that version to someone else and then marry quickly, the actual marriage can bring many unpleasant surprises. Hopefully this chapter has given you some wise directions that will help you get to know your boyfriend or girlfriend well enough that you can reasonably trust that moving forward will be a blessing to both of you as well as honoring to Jesus.

But it's also true that people can and do have long-lasting and loving marriages without doing all that is suggested in this chapter. We cannot possibly know what will happen five, ten, or twenty years from now. People can change after they marry for the better. Some grow and mature at a steady rate over time. Many relationships truly get better with age.

So it's important to look at what trajectory you are both on and what trajectory your relationship is on. Do you see growth in yourself and your significant other in the areas mentioned in this chapter? The most important quality for change to happen is humility. If you raise these issues, are your concerns received with humility? And if concerns are raised with you, do you receive them with humility? Remember that wherever you are right now, going to Jesus for forgiveness and help is what will change you.

Reflection Questions

1. Talk to two couples who have been married for at least ten years. Ask how well they knew each other, what they wished they would have known, and how they work together to have the joy and peace they currently experience.
2. Write a list of situations you would like to experience alongside your boyfriend or girlfriend to see how they respond. Why did you choose those situations? What concerns were you trying to assuage or confirm?
3. Study Romans 5:1–5 along with James 1:2–4. Write a few paragraphs on how you believe past pressure has grown you to be who you are today. How has understanding your core identity in Jesus helped you to trust his plans? What two areas do you know need maturing?
4. Skim the book of Job. Look for the increasing intensity of the friends' accusations and the growing intensity of Job's justification. Have you seen this dynamic in your life where increasing pressure results in sinful responses? What lessons can you learn from the Lord's response in Job 38–42 that will help you with that struggle? Why might learning these lessons be an important part of moving toward engagement?

Chapter 5
Address Individual Issues Individually

> **The Big Idea:** You're ready to take the next step in your relationship when each of you is committed to love, care, and encourage the other. This happens when you have both worked through your struggles (or are working through them) by depending on Jesus, his Word, and his people. If you or your boyfriend or girlfriend bring significant unresolved matters to a marriage, whether due to past sin or suffering, that will make married life surprisingly difficult. Wisdom means being willing to wait for the next step of engagement until each of you is willing to address these matters individually.

A FEW YEARS ago, I was asked to counsel a couple from another city who as having serious marriage issues. Their marital problems were complicated by how it was affecting their children. They shared a sad story of regular conflict that grew more frequent and intense over time, and it included the husband's sexual unfaithfulness. Early in our counseling, he said that the root cause of their marriage struggles was communication problems.

Sadly, he was completely wrong. While he was right that they had communication struggles, he was wrong to consider this the root cause, since God says that words flow from the heart (Matthew 15:19; Luke 6:45; James 4:1–2). He had also been involved sexually with different women for ten years prior to meeting his wife. How could his immoral behavior be caused by their poor communication?

He never admitted his responsibility in their struggles, and eventually they stopped coming for counseling. I have occasionally wondered what happened to his wife and their children. What ways did she continue to suffer? Did she stay in the marriage and endure, or did they divorce? I am sure their children are grown and starting families of their own by now. But how were they affected?

I also wondered if anything could have been done years earlier that could have prevented the heartache. This story is a cautionary tale that highlights the importance of each person addressing their own issues before engagement so that they will be ready to love, care for, and serve their spouse. Of course, you can't expect the person you marry to be perfect. But I wonder if the story could have turned out differently if the wife had trusted mentor and accountability relationships that could have alerted her to red flags about her future husband, whether his (presumed) unwillingness to share deeply about his past or an avoidance of his own close Christian relationships, or any other signs that he wasn't healthy in his relationship with Christ.

Significant personal issues don't automatically demand the end of a relationship. A lot depends on the response you get when these issues are raised. It's a red flag when someone responds defensively with excuses, blame-shifting, and claims that they can handle the issue on their own. Conversely, when someone responds with humility and a willingness to ask for and receive help, that should encourage both of you. This has happened with couples I counseled. One couple actually postponed their wedding because they had personal matters that were best addressed individually. They knew that to be ready to care for another, they needed the Lord to work in specific ways in their heart. Once those issues stabilized, the date was set, and they moved forward in joy. This is a perfect example of what this chapter advises.

Significant Areas of Chronic Struggle

It's fair to ask, What areas should we handle on our own before we are ready to move forward in our relationship? I can't provide you with a comprehensive list. Instead, I suggest that you talk to the most important people in your life, such as parents, mentors, siblings, or pastors and ask their advice. Some battles are easier to fight than others. Some battles have more serious consequences than others. While there are other issues that could be just as challenging, the following three areas have consistently arisen in my counseling, and they're perhaps most challenging due to their intermittent nature.

A chronic struggle with drinking too much

> And do not get drunk with wine, for that is dissipation, but be filled with the Spirit, speaking to one another in psalms and hymns and spiritual songs, singing and making melody with your heart to the Lord. (Ephesians 5:18–19)

Perhaps your girlfriend drinks too much (i.e., to the point of visible intoxication) once a month or so. If you raise that as a problem with her, it would be good if she repented, asked you to pray for her, and then sought help from others as well. But what should you do if she says it's fine for her to drink too much since it's only once in a while? What if she doesn't want you to discuss her drinking with her or anyone else? Those are all red flags.

The boyfriend or girlfriend who gets hammered after a stressful week will have stressful weeks in the future. Is alcohol their functional god when times are tough? Is alcohol better than the promises of Scripture and living to declare how awesome Jesus is? I have met spouses who, with tears in their eyes, were at a loss because their husband or wife hid alcohol in water bottles, drove their little children while drunk, and then blamed their spouse for their drinking. Take this issue seriously now; perhaps your concern will be what God uses to help your boyfriend or girlfriend address this struggle.

A chronic struggle with laziness

> How long will you lie down, O sluggard? When will you arise from your sleep? "A little sleep, a little slumber, A little folding of the hands to rest"— Your poverty will come in like a vagabond And your need like an armed man. (Proverbs 6:9–11)

> The sluggard says, "There is a lion outside; I will be killed in the streets!" (Proverbs 22:13)

We often hear about work-life balance—and that is a good thing. Abusive workplace practices have resulted in child-labor laws, federal safety standards, and unions. But that isn't an excuse for not working hard or being faithful to whatever God is calling us to do. The person who makes up excuses for why they can't get things done is someone that the Bible calls "lazy." Learning how to work hard and be responsible is rarely inherent. We learn and grow through pressure. As a father, my goal was to help my children learn to work hard. They may or may not make a large income, but if they are faithful workers, they will always have a job.

But what happens when your boyfriend or girlfriend does not like to work? Do you hear excuses like, "I might get my hands dirty," I don't want to get sweaty," "I have plenty of time to do this tomorrow," or "I work so hard in school; I just want a break"? Excuses are warning signs. They might not seem like a big deal now, but what happens if they don't grow and mature over the next ten years? Look for signs of growth on these issues.

A chronic struggle with pornography

> But immorality or any impurity or greed must not even be named among you, as is proper among saints. (Ephesians 5:3)

Pornography is one of the most prevalent issues in our world, and it affects both Christians and non-Christians. Pornography used to be thought of as a predominantly male issue, but it affects both sexes. Boyfriends or girlfriends who think that pornography struggles will end after marriage are deceived. While decreases in intensity and frequency are positive signs, it is sometimes difficult to tell whether a person has turned from that sin. I have sat with many married couples where one spouse is devastated that the other has returned to pornography. While 1 Corinthians 7:1–5 reminds us that married persons help each other with temptation, this cannot be used to excuse behavior or to argue that the problem will be resolved after marriage.

I have counseled young women and men to end relationships with their boyfriends or girlfriends if these struggles are consistent or life-dominating. Marriage is hard—and it becomes even harder if you are married to a drunk, a slacker, or someone who consistently struggles with pornography and masturbation. Instead, encourage them to get help and to own their sin, and then see what happens. If they do, you might have found the right person. A spouse who loves the Lord in good times and owns their sinfulness through repentance is someone you can build a life with.

Past Sexual Violence or Trauma

The previous section focused on sinful habits and behavior that should be addressed prior to the engagement ring. Another area to consider, with patience and gentleness, is how past sexual violence might have affected your boyfriend or girlfriend.

Some events cause suffering in ways that many would find shocking. My friend who serves in law enforcement once told me that they arrested a father who trafficked his own daughter. He actually lived in my neighborhood. Who knows the impact this horrible suffering had on her and what scars she will carry.

Not everyone responds to events, even terrible events, in the same way. Some are able to move forward sooner than others. If your boyfriend or girlfriend has experienced sexual violence or other forms of trauma, then your compassion may not be enough. You might be sensitive, caring, loving, and a good listener. You might say that you are willing to help them through the challenging and long-lasting struggle. These are all God-glorifying actions, but they do not mean your loved one is ready or able to work through their suffering.

Joseph's story is one of many stories in the Bible about someone suffering deep trauma (see Genesis 37–50). Joseph is trafficked by his brothers, sold as a slave, taken to a different country, propositioned by his master's wife, lied about, sent to prison, and forgotten. Yet God does not forget Joseph, and eventually he becomes the right-hand man of Egypt's ruler and is used by God to save his family from famine. Years later, when Joseph is reunited with his family, he forgives his brothers. But they still feel guilty about what they had done. When their father, Jacob, dies, they are afraid that Joseph will at last seek his revenge. Here's what happens when they approach Joseph:

> When Joseph's brothers saw that their father was dead, they said, "What if Joseph bears a grudge against us and pays us back in full for all the wrong which we did to him!" So they sent *a message* to Joseph, saying, "Your father charged before he died, saying, 'Thus you shall say to Joseph, "Please forgive, I beg you, the transgression of your brothers and their sin, for they did you wrong."' And now, please forgive the transgression of

> the servants of the God of your father." And Joseph wept when they spoke to him. Then his brothers also came and fell down before him and said, "Behold, we are your servants." But Joseph said to them, "Do not be afraid, for am I in God's place? As for you, you meant evil against me, *but* God meant it for good in order to bring about this present result, to preserve many people alive. So therefore, do not be afraid; I will provide for you and your little ones." So he comforted them and spoke kindly to them. (Genesis 50:15–21)

Despite the many years that have passed, the brothers fully expect Joseph to take revenge. Now that their father Jacob is dead, Joseph has no constraints on his treatment of his brothers. The brothers understood that time alone does not heal wounds. In fact, sometimes it makes them worse. Yet, God's grace is still sufficient to break through and provide all the resources necessary to live a productive and fulfilling life. That is how Joseph responds. He forgives them and reassures them that his forgiveness comes from his trust in God. No doubt, this took time and trust in the Lord for Joseph to be able to say. Your boyfriend or girlfriend might not be ready for that right now.

Wise is the person who is willing to acknowledge the hurts and receive help to address them. This will allow each person to be ready for the ring and ultimately ready to embrace the sacrifice required to love and serve another person. Once again, it takes wisdom to know if your boyfriend or girlfriend is ready for a committed relationship or whether they need to pause to address their own suffering and hurt. You can support them by encouraging them to talk with a pastor or a counselor and also pray with and for them for healing from the Spirit. But mostly you will need to be patient with the trajectory of healing that can be slow and halting.

What should you do if you don't see them able or willing to seek counsel and help? I would advise you to pause your plans for moving forward toward engagement, but I would also encourage you to speak with those who are close to you to get their input.

A Former Marriage or Children from a Former Relationship

While this might not be a common issue among those in their early to mid-twenties, it is not unusual among older singles. It is fair to ask about the role of a former marriage or a child from a former relationship. There might be various stories about past relationships, and some might be more problematic than others. All these situations require wisdom to navigate. For example, someone with a former spouse may or may not be ready to learn from their previous relationship. Some might not be willing to acknowledge and discuss the long-term challenges associated with a blended family. Some may have experienced years of navigating custody challenges, dual parenting, or relationship dynamics that change over time.

When someone has been married previously or has children from a previous relationship, it is best to ensure that each person has independently worked through any past experiences and is ready for another relationship. This will be challenging, but it will be much better over the long run. Once again, getting help from a mentor, pastor, or counselor is a good way forward.

What's Your Trajectory?

I want you to experience the blessings of planning a wedding, doing premarital counseling, and ultimately enjoying your marriage. At the same time, some move forward to engagement and marriage without recognizing that they have some concerns to address first. Remember the gospel of Jesus Christ—it's all about forgiveness, healing, and becoming more like Jesus as we follow him. So there is hope for all! Again, the goal is not perfection, but a trajectory facing toward Jesus. Discuss with your mentor how to balance not being perfect with the goal of a track record of faithful resistance to temptation.

Those who have sinned greatly can be forgiven greatly, and those who have suffered incredible harm can rise from the ashes stronger and godlier than ever. We praise the Lord for every trophy of his grace.

Reflection Questions

1. Take stock of your own life. Is there a habitual or intermittent sin that, if continued in marriage, could destroy it? Is there an area of suffering that you have chosen not to address but that you know needs attention prior to engagement? If so, please discuss your concerns with your mentor and with your significant other.
2. Take stock of your significant other's life. Create a list of questions you have about your boyfriend or girlfriend, or consider what struggles would be a big deal to you if you discovered them after marriage.
3. Read the passages from this chapter and memorize the one that resonates with you the most. Why did you choose that passage?
4. Read Joseph's whole story (Genesis 37–50). What things did Joseph believe about God that enabled him to function amid deep suffering? What did Joseph do because of those beliefs? Although Joseph's response to his brothers came many years later, can you see yourself moving in that direction? Do you have someone you trust will listen to your story without judgment and help you turn to the Lord in your suffering?

Chapter 6
Respecting Standards, Commitments, and Opinions

> **The Big Idea:** You both have standards, commitments, and opinions about how a dating relationship should proceed. It is loving and honoring to Jesus when you both follow the example of Jesus, who put others' interests ahead of his own.

TOM AND SUSIE had been married for five years when they sought help for their relationship. As I heard their story, it became clear that Tom had a history of failing to respect Susie. Tom successfully justified his actions and created pain and hurt that followed them into the marriage, and she was struggling with bitterness toward him. When Susie was sixteen, she made a commitment to remain sexually pure until she was married. However, in college, Susie was date-raped. She grieved the violent theft of her virginity. During that vulnerable time, she met Tom. Tom was nice in many ways, but he pressed Susie's physical boundaries until she gave in to his desires. Although they married, the relationship began on the wrong footing with Tom pressing Susie to change her standard, commitments, and opinions.

By contrast, consider Joe and Karen. Karen had been promiscuous prior to her conversion, but when she trusted Christ at seventeen, the Lord changed her. Knowing her past, Karen wanted almost no physical affection. She knew how easy it would be to move from a gentle kiss to a displeasing action to her Savior. Joe did not hold to the same convictions; he thought it might be nice to kiss and snuggle while watching a movie. However, Joe decided that loving Karen would mean relinquishing his desire for affection and waiting until marriage. He decided that Jesus would be most pleased if he helped her keep her commitment in the way she thought was best. Joe and Karen are now married and enjoying a loving marriage. One way that Joe showed his character, his commitment to Jesus, and his love for Karen was by respecting her standards, commitments, and opinions.

In chapter 4, we acknowledged that it is difficult to learn what a person will be like in a marriage relationship because you can't totally replicate it without being married. We can learn, study, and discuss various matters, but some things will not be revealed until marriage. We also discussed the truth that until you're married (not just engaged), you are an individual person. You are free to make the decisions you want to make. This chapter looks at the same issue from a different perspective. We are going to consider the place of standards, commitments, and opinions.

While each of you is your own person, moving to engagement is a major step in the direction of oneness. The engagement period is a time to prepare for marriage—it's not for deciding whether to be married. You are deciding *now*. So when you're considering whether to buy a ring or say yes to a proposal, where does respecting your own and your boyfriend's or girlfriend's standards, commitments, and opinions come into play?

A Warning for Women

> Blessings are on the head of the righteous,
> But the mouth of the wicked conceals violence.
> (Proverbs 10:6)
>
> An angry man stirs up strife,
> And a hot-tempered man abounds in transgression.
> (Proverbs 29:22)

Let's begin with a warning for the women who are reading this book. Imagine that you and your boyfriend have established written physical standards for your relationship. You wear a purity ring given to you by your father. You and your parents have encouraged you to have a "less is more" attitude toward physical affection. Thus, you decided before the Lord that kissing is the furthest you will go until marriage. Your boyfriend faithfully keeps that line—until one day he doesn't. Suddenly, that is not far enough. Even after your objections, he continues to try to push you past your standards.

You might be tempted to justify his actions, thinking that he is expressing his love and attraction for you and "just can't help it." Since it is always nice to be wanted and loved, you dismiss it as a small flaw in an overall great man. You might be right. Maybe he is untaught, immature, or in need of significant Christian growth, which will happen soon. Maybe this moment of trying to go past your standards is a wake-up call that the Lord will use to create growth.

However, there are many Christian women, maybe even in your church, who would strongly urge you to end the relationship. They live under the heavy weight of a husband who is always right, knows no boundaries, justifies his actions, and manipulates them later with words of love.

Proverbs warns us that violence, or the potential for violence, is often concealed. Like sin itself, your boyfriend might be using kind words as a smoke screen for his real heart. Even those who have been married or in relationships before might fall into this trap.

Imagine a single mother working hard to provide, and her boyfriend telling her that she shouldn't need to carry the burden alone anymore. He would like to help. Such words are powerful, but they could be deceitful, hiding the wickedness that will be revealed later. In the worst of cases, this man might combine his pride with explosive, sinful anger and become violent.

A Warning for Men

> It is better to live in a corner of a roof
> Than in a house shared with a contentious woman.
> (Proverbs 21:9)

> It is better to live in a desert land
> Than with a contentious and vexing woman.
> (Proverbs 21:19)

Men, please heed these passages because they are warnings to you. This warning may not look the same as pushing through physical standards, although that is possible. More common is a scenario where your opinions or commitments don't seem to matter. Your girlfriend might be smart and competent. On the one hand, you love that about her. You look forward to the day when you can combine your gifts, skills, and competencies to accomplish far more for Jesus than what either of you could do alone.

However, there is a potential dark side. Instead of wanting to engage, be part of the process, and work together, you notice that your opinions only matter to her when they agree with her opinions. Your commitments are okay so long as they do not conflict with hers. When questioned, she justifies herself with accomplishments and maybe even a track record of making decisions. You decide it's better to just agree. Perhaps you think, *Nobody's perfect* or *Happy wife, happy life*. While sometimes you are hurt by her negative attitude toward what you think, agreeing with her keeps the peace. You excuse it without thinking about the possible long-term ramifications.

Proverbs 21:9 and 19 are warnings to men about being with difficult women. Many homes in Old Testament times had a flat room and some even had a room on the roof. Solomon warned men that contentious women are so difficult that it would be better to live on the corner of the roof. Verse 19 continues the theme, saying it is better to live in a desert. What you excuse in dating may grow to a level where you would rather not be in your own home. Instead of being the servant leader of your home, you feel like you are barely welcome.

Heed the Warning Signs

Men and women, these biblical warnings are real because these situations happen. I have seen marriages made difficult by both angry men and angry women. I have counseled them, and I have hurt for my friends. Often the warning signs were present, but they were not heeded.

One of the worst examples of this occurred during my junior year of high school when I met Kelly in world history class. We sat next to each other in the back of the class, and the more time I spent with her, the more I liked her. But there was one problem—she had a boyfriend who treated her terribly. When I asked her about his behavior and why she tolerated it, she justified his actions. Even though he yelled at her, pushed her, demanded sex, and tried to control her, she refused to give him up. The whole situation made me sad. She was a victim of sexual and physical violence and couldn't seem to break that cycle. I hope that eventually she trusted Jesus as her Savior, dumped her abusive boyfriend, and found someone who would treasure her.

You should expect far different behavior from your boyfriend or girlfriend. If you are ignoring clear warning signs, then you may deeply regret that decision later.

Standards, Commitments, and Opinions to Respect

Hopefully you are not dealing with any of the serious issues that were just raised. But take some time to think about what commitments you have made and what commitments your boyfriend or girlfriend have made that are worthy of respect from one another. What might those be? Here's a sample list:

- *Standards on physical, intimate contact.* Often one person in the relationship has made a commitment to place voluntary boundaries around their physical activity to learn more about the other person, focus on their character, and remove unnecessary temptation to sin. If you do not have the same conviction, can you accept your boyfriend's or girlfriend's standard? If you hold the tighter standard, does your boyfriend or girlfriend accept and respect that standard?
- *Prior commitments to a job, education, or ministry.* When Stephanie and I were dating, she believed that the Lord wanted her to complete her nursing degree. It was part of a commitment she made years before I was in the picture. Since I was a little older and further in my education, it would have been easy for me to justify encouraging her to quit, but I didn't. We married prior to her graduation. Once married, the pressure of being in school, being a wife, and having a part-time job resulted in tears nearly every evening. Something had to go. What would it be? It would have been easy to justify the need for the job. However, her roles as a wife and a student remained commitments to the Lord, and we both needed to honor them. So she quit her job. Be careful to not end a commitment just to secure a relationship. This might result in a long-standing pattern of commitment-breaking and lead to a life of chaos and not honoring Jesus.

- *Personal opinions.* Do you respect each other's opinions and preferences, even when they're different from yours? Do either of you pressure the other to do something you don't want to do? These are all important questions to ask about yourself and your significant other. Of course, you are not looking for total agreement on every issue. Instead, you are looking for someone who can respect and accept differences in opinions and preferences and not pressure you to change.

Jesus talks about this in Matthew 5:33–37 when he says,

> "Again, you have heard that the ancients were told, 'You shall not make false vows, but shall fulfill your vows to the Lord.' But I say to you, make no oath at all, either by heaven, for it is the throne of God, or by the earth, for it is the footstool of His feet, or by Jerusalem, for it is the city of the great King. Nor shall you make an oath by your head, for you cannot make one hair white or black. But let your statement be, 'Yes, yes' *or* 'No, no'; anything beyond these is of evil."

This passage reminds us to let our word be our bond and to respect others' vows or decisions about what they believe God is calling them to do. If you learn that your boyfriend or girlfriend has committed to serve in a ministry, then if you are going to be together, you should help them keep that commitment and perhaps even serve alongside them.

New Testament "One Anothers"

This chapter started with warnings, but now let's look at this subject more positively. In the New Testament, there are many passages known as the "one anothers." They describe the way that believers should respond to one another. Let's consider three of them.

Encourage one another

> Therefore encourage one another and build up one another, just as you also are doing. (1 Thessalonians 5:11)

The Thessalonian church struggled to understand end-time theology. Paul instructs them in his letter, and then he tells them that they should mutually encourage each other. Doubts or fears might arise for various reasons, but truth sets one free and comforts the soul. Do you encourage each other with the truths of Scripture? If your conversations involve discussions about how the Lord and his Word help you, then this is a good sign to move forward in your relationship.

Accept one another just as Christ accepted you

> Therefore, accept one another, just as Christ also accepted us to the glory of God. (Romans 15:7)

The early church struggled to develop unity and love between Jewish and Gentile believers. The Jews' historical relationship to God, their connection to the old covenant, and common matters like pride and favoritism resulted in division. Not every struggle between them involved a theological right and wrong. This chapter emphasizes opinions, commitments, and standards. Some of these might be theological convictions, but others could be preference. Can you maintain unity even when there are differences of opinion, standards, or commitments? If so, wonderful. You should be thankful. If, however, they result in arguments, attempts to push boundaries, and lack of respect for the other person, then you may have some concerns to address before moving forward.

Honor one another above yourselves

> *Be* devoted to one another in brotherly love; give preference to one another in honor. (Romans 12:10)

Some relationships show early signs of trouble because one person always wants the credit. Consider that this could be an indication of self-centeredness that may be challenging in the future. Instead, your future spouse should show you honor and not seek it for themselves, even if you are not acting honorably. We should talk about the good publicly and deal with the challenges in private. If you and your significant other are quick to give or share honor and slow to desire it, then you might be ready for the ring.

What's Your Trajectory?

This chapter looked at your relationship through the lens of standards, opinions, and commitments. How you deal with differences will provide a window into the spiritual health of your relationship. The "one another" passages in the New Testament all point to how we express in our relationships the grace we have been given in Jesus. In Christ, God accepts us, encourages us, and treats us with honor as his dearly loved children, so we share that grace with others. Do you see yourself and your significant other growing in these things? When you both are growing in living out the "one anothers" of the New Testament, your relationship is in a good place to move forward.

Reflection Questions

1. Write out the standards you hold to and the commitments you have made along with your reasons for them. Can you do the same for your significant other?
2. Consider what it would look like for your boyfriend or girlfriend to encourage, accept, or honor the standards you set,

the commitments you have to the Lord, and the opinions that matter to you. Consider the same for yourself.

3. Skim the warning section of this chapter again. Discuss with your mentor whether any of these items exist that you have chosen to ignore at this point. If they exist, discuss how you could start a conversation with your boyfriend or girlfriend to address them.
4. Look at some of the key "one another" passages in the Bible. Here is a list to get you started in addition to the ones discussed in the chapter:

   - Love one another: "A new commandment I give to you, that you love one another, even as I have loved you" (John 13:34, 15:12; Romans 12:10; 1 Peter 4:8).
   - Serve and submit: "Through love serve one another" (Galatians 5:13); "Submit to one another out of reverence for Christ" (Ephesians 5:21 NIV).
   - Encourage and build up: "Encourage one another and build up one another" (1 Thessalonians 5:11); "Spur one another on toward love and good deeds" (Hebrews 10:24 NIV).
   - Forgive and bear burdens: "Forgiving each other" (Ephesians 4:32; Colossians 3:13); "Bear one another's burdens" (Galatians 6:2).
   - Honor and accept: "Honor one another above yourselves" (Romans 12:10 NIV), and "Accept one another, just as Christ also accepted you" (Romans 15:7).

Evaluate yourself on a scale of 1–10. For example, Encourage one another = 7/10; Accept one another = 9/10. Include a brief explanation ("I respect my girlfriend, but her commitment to refrain from physical contact past a simple kiss is hard for me to accept.").

Chapter 7
Be Willing to Resolve Problems

> **The Big Idea:** Long-term relationships will have problems to resolve. In Jesus-honoring relationships, you solve problems together as you rely on Jesus. Relationships where problems are ignored, minimized, or unresolved eventually struggle.

TIM AND JULIE argued almost every day. They could not remember most of the reasons. As we talked, they shared that they both grew up in families that pretended problems did not exist. So during their dating and premarital counseling, they did not acknowledge or confront any of their problems. Looking back, they realized that they did have problems, but they were masters at ignoring them—at least for a while. Now that they could no longer ignore issues, their problems were apparent, yet they had no tools for resolving them.

Tim and Julie are like a lot of couples. They did not have any major issues early on and so continued the bad patterns they learned while growing up. They couldn't believe the difference it made to learn that the Lord Jesus provides everything we need to solve challenges together. They are now able to resolve their problems quickly and experience the joy of living together in harmony.

Premarital counseling normally emphasizes problem-solving. Being able to resolve problems and issues in a mature Christian fashion makes for a strong and durable marriage, and it's also important to your dating relationship. I hope that you have both been encouraged as you've worked through this book. I am also thankful that you were willing to invest the time and effort into carefully thinking through your relationship. Dating couples experience differing amounts of problems, so you may only have had to work through a few issues together, but be assured that if your relationship continues, you will have the opportunity to work through more.

Everyone struggles with immaturity, weakness, and sin. Proverbs was not written only to make the immature wise but also to make the wise wiser (Proverbs 1:1–7). There is no end to maturing and gaining wisdom. When I study Proverbs today, I ask different questions than I did when I was twenty, thirty, or forty. We are also weak. Being weak does not mean we are sinful. It means that we cannot do what others can do, that we have learning limitations (not everyone can be a rocket scientist), or that we have limited experiences. And we struggle with sin. How we deal with our sins and the sins of someone we love is a key part of having a lasting relationship.

In the book of Hebrews, we are called to lay aside the sin that can easily entangle us and every encumbrance (or barrier) that stands in the way of becoming like Jesus. We must fix our eyes on Jesus, remembering and thanking God for all that he has done and now does for us (Hebrews 12:1–2). Being able to solve problems is one of the fruits of a life founded on Jesus's love for us and the good news that our sins are forgiven. When you know that you have been forgiven much, you love much (Luke 7:47). Love is expressed in humility before God and before each other. Let's consider some ways you can assess your (and your partner's) ability to resolve problems.

Willingness to Accept Responsibility

> "Why do you look at the speck that is in your brother's eye, but do not notice the log that is in your own eye? Or how can you say to your brother, 'Let me take the speck out of your eye,' and behold, the log is in your own eye? You hypocrite, first take the log out of your own eye, and then you will see clearly to take the speck out of your brother's eye. (Matthew 7:3–5)

Problems cannot be resolved if no one accepts responsibility. But that is not our natural bent. When confronted, we are tempted to justify, rationalize, defend ourselves or our reputation, and try to get the other person to admit wrong. As you are dating, you should see your boyfriend or girlfriend owning their sin without needing to ensure the other person understands theirs. You should also see this in yourself. Verse 5 explains why it is so important to take the log out of our own eye—because only then we will see clearly. Those who refuse to own their responsibility for their sins are and will be increasingly difficult to live with.

You could look at this through the lens of pride and humility. Humble people are willing to look at themselves, while those stuck in pride look to put the blame on someone or something else. Taking responsibility is not only a matter of words; it includes action steps appropriate to the offense.

Patterns of consistent blame-shifting, ignoring real issues by refusing to talk about them, or making excuses do not normally resolve themselves. Marriage usually makes them worse. In a dating relationship, you should see a willingness to acknowledge wrongdoing in your life and in your boyfriend's or girlfriend's life.

Willingness to Repent of Sin

> "Be on your guard! If your brother sins, rebuke him; and if he repents, forgive him. And if he sins against

> you seven times a day, and returns to you seven times, saying, 'I repent,' forgive him." The apostles said to the Lord, "Increase our faith!" (Luke 17:3–5)
>
> "So, King Agrippa, I did not prove disobedient to the heavenly vision, but *kept* declaring both to those of Damascus first, and *also* at Jerusalem and *then* throughout all the region of Judea, and *even* to the Gentiles, that they should repent and turn to God, performing deeds appropriate to repentance." (Acts 26:19–20)

Repentance can be one of the most difficult actions to assess because it has both an inner and an outer component. Simply put, repentance is turning away from sin and turning toward righteousness. Since we are weak and our repentance is not perfect, a war still exists in our hearts between what God calls us to do and what we naturally want to do. Thankfully, Jesus has paid with his death for all our sins, so when we ask for forgiveness from God, we can be sure that we will be forgiven. The gift of being forgiven gives us the power to repent and also to forgive those who have sinned against us.

Let's imagine that a woman is dating a man who exhibits sinful anger. She confronts his anger, and he responds by asking her for forgiveness. That sounds good, and it might be. It is far better than accusing her or blaming it on his Irish heritage or red hair or some other excuse. Here is where it gets complicated: We should also expect his expressions of anger to progressively change. Repentance should result in a decrease in intensity and frequency, but that does not mean instant perfection. That's what Paul means in Acts when he talks about performing deeds in keeping with our repentance. A changed heart results in a changed life. But, of course, this is a process. Are you seeing progress in yourself? How about in your significant other?

Let's also imagine that a man is dating a woman who tries to control him and complains when she doesn't get her way. He confronts her controlling nature. She responds by asking for forgiveness. Once again, this is a great response! But is she changing, or is she using the right words to manipulate her boyfriend? We would not expect that this one moment would suddenly change a pattern of control, but are we seeing the intensity and frequency decline? What is the trajectory?

As a church leader, I am occasionally required, along with other leaders, to assess whether a person is repentant. It is one of the most difficult aspects of pastoral ministry. Some Bible passages state that the words "I repent" trigger forgiveness, and yet other times, the lack of fruit is an indication of the manipulative heart. How can you tell the difference?

Time can be helpful here. Character is revealed over time. As you carefully pay attention to your boyfriend's or girlfriend's words and behavior, you should gain confidence that when repentance occurs, things get better. If that is so, wonderful! You should be encouraged that you are dating a person who is genuinely willing to repent.

But let's consider another possibility. What happens when you confront them multiple times, and you still see the same concerns? He is still exhibiting sinful anger, and she is still controlling. This is when repentance is ever more difficult to judge. If this is a genuine concern for either of you, then I highly recommend biblical counseling. Slow down and discuss your concerns in person with someone who has experience.

Willingness to Forgive

> Seek the Lord while He may be found; Call upon Him while He is near. Let the wicked forsake his way And the unrighteous man his thoughts; And let him return to the Lord, And He will have compassion on him, And

> to our God, For He will abundantly pardon. "For My thoughts are not your thoughts, Nor are your ways My ways," declares the Lord. "For *as* the heavens are higher than the earth, So are My ways higher than your ways And My thoughts than your thoughts." (Isaiah 55:6–9)

> Be kind to one another, tender-hearted, forgiving each other, just as God in Christ also has forgiven you. (Ephesians 4:32)

Although believers often use this passage in Isaiah to explain why certain hard things happen in their life, it is primarily about how God forgives us when we would be tempted to withhold forgiveness, stay bitter, and hold a grudge. We need to be like the Lord—ready to forgive and reconcile with those who have sinned against us.

Ephesians 4:32 provides the motivation for forgiveness. When individuals look at forgiveness through horizontal relationships, it seems impossible—our hurts feel too big and our desire to get even can be overwhelming.

But when we start with our vertical relationship with God, we remember how much we have been forgiven. We remember that God forgives us for a debt far greater than anyone's debt to us (Matthew 18:21–35). Because of our great gratitude for how God has forgiven us, we can forgive those who sin against us. We forgive because we have been forgiven.

Couples struggle when God's forgiveness for them, through Jesus, does not really fill them with thankfulness. Instead, they remain mired in wanting their relationship to be "fair." The most extreme example I've seen occurred when one spouse committed adultery, and in response the other did the same, proclaiming, "Now we are even." It is not surprising that their relationship didn't last. The Lord wants something better for us. He wants us to forgive because we have been forgiven.

Forgiveness is easier (sometimes) when the offenses are small. Maybe your sins and hurts against each other have been small. Small enough, in fact, that you could ignore them without it being a major deal for either of you. However, learning to forgive small offenses produces the Christlike character necessary to forgive larger ones. It is like developing muscle memory. The more you repent of your wrongs and freely forgive the wrongs of your boyfriend or girlfriend, the better you will be at doing it.

Not only does this honor Jesus, but it can also serve as protection against more damaging actions in the future. Your dating relationship might not be characterized by challenge, conflict, or sinfulness. Praise the Lord! However, learning to repent and forgive is necessary for a lifelong relationship filled with joy.

Move Forward with Joy

> Not that I have already obtained *it* or have already become perfect, but I press on so that I may lay hold of that for which also I was laid hold of by Christ Jesus. Brethren, I do not regard myself as having laid hold of *it* yet; but one thing *I do*: forgetting what *lies* behind and reaching forward to what *lies* ahead, I press on toward the goal for the prize of the upward call of God in Christ Jesus. (Philippians 3:12–14)

The final aspect of problem-solving is moving forward with joy. Paul recounts some of his past in Philippians 3, including the part that was not so good (see v. 6). He is neither overwhelmed by his past nor using his current success to justify quitting. He always presses on toward his goal. Football commentators will sometimes mention that players need a short memory to be successful. They forget about the fumble, interception, or missed opportunity so they can treat each new play as an opportunity for success.

What about in your relationship? Once a person truly repents, can you move forward with joy? Or does the hurt, pain, and fear linger, keeping you from moving forward? When people can't move forward in joy, it may indicate a lack of forgiveness. If you are seeing that in your relationship, then you should discuss this further with your mentor. You may be helped by reflecting on God's promises that he removes our sins as far as the east is from the west (Psalm 103:12), or that he remembers our sins no more. Jesus's cross moves us from the kingdom of darkness to his kingdom of light (Hebrews 8:12). Remembering that he became sin for us so that we can become the righteousness of God (2 Corinthians 5:21) can be a powerful motivator to move forward with joy, knowing that as you forgive, you are sharing the forgiveness you have been given.

Learning a lesson means we understand where we went wrong, we reconciled whatever harm we did in the process, and we know the danger points moving forward. It does not mean dwelling on or being hindered by the past. Once forgiven, we live in freedom and should not be plagued by guilt. I realize this is easier said than done. That's one reason it is helpful for you to keep short accounts even with small problems. If one of you is often late or has a habit of saying things that hurt the other's feelings, that may not be a relationship stopper. You could forget about it and move on. But the practice of forgiveness and keeping short accounts will help you exercise this truth when the stakes are higher.

What's Your Trajectory?

I hope you have experienced the joy of moving forward after sin. I hope you have recognized and solved your relationship problem, and now you are enjoying being reconciled. Even if you are dealing with little problems, learning to solve them quickly through taking responsibility, repenting, forgiving, and moving forward is a great sign that your relationship might be ready for the next step. Are you taking small steps toward being able to speak honestly and listen to one another? Are you both growing in learning to forgive as Christ has forgiven you? If yes, you might be ready for the ring. If problem-solving has been challenging for you, then this is a good time to talk to your mentor about larger spiritual matters. It may be that focusing on appreciating the cross, valuing the righteousness of Christ added to your account, lamenting failures or patterns you learned from others, or understanding more about your identity in Christ could result in the change necessary to solve problems biblically.

Reflection Questions

1. Describe a time in your relationship when you needed to ask for forgiveness. Did you specifically identify the sin? Did you ask for forgiveness or simply state that you did something wrong? Were you ready to move forward in joy?
2. Describe a time in your relationship that your boyfriend or girlfriend needed to ask for forgiveness. Did they specifically identify the sin? Did they ask for forgiveness or simply state that they did something wrong? Were they ready to move forward in joy?
3. Discuss with your mentor what you learned about how you solve problems. Do you ignore them and hope things will get better? Are you quick to repent without prompting? Are you willing to listen to a confrontation?
4. Write a list of any problems that exist in your relationship that have remained hidden or unresolved. Discuss with your mentor what prevented you from resolving them, what steps would be required to resolve them, and what relational dynamics might be at play resulting in unresolved issues.

Chapter 8
Seek the Encouragement of Family and Friends

> **The Big Idea:** We should seek the encouragement and counsel of those who are closest to us and love us the most. These trusted voices, who have our best interest in mind, can help us see what we might miss or overlook.

A wise man will hear and increase in learning,
And a man of understanding will acquire wise counsel.
(PROVERBS 1:5)

Oil and perfume make the heart glad,
So a man's counsel is sweet to his friend.
(PROVERBS 27:9)

WHEN OUR SONS were serious about women, we wanted to be involved. We thought it would be a great opportunity to support our sons and celebrate their growing relationship. Since we knew our sons, we also wanted to get to know their girlfriends. The Lord blessed both sons with women who are perfect for them. But I have watched as other parents and friends noticed significant issues in their children's relationships but did not feel free to speak into them. And of course, with our adult children, it's usually best to be invited to comment before we do. Are you willing to invite those who know you best to speak into your relationship?

God designed us to be in relationship with him and one another, so it should not be surprising that relationships feel good. This does not change after the wedding. Spouses want to be loved and wanted too. I want my wife to want to spend time with me, talk to me, ask advice, be affectionate, celebrate, grieve, and experience all of life together. We want attention because we were made for it.

This is all wonderful, but sometimes we can be so caught up in feeling loved and wanted that we miss important issues that need our attention. That's why we need help from others, who can help us discern if we are really ready for the ring.

Proverbs reminds us that missing important truths is part of our everyday human experience. We are not all-knowing. Proverbs 1:5 is part of a larger introduction to the book that runs from verses 1 through 7. In it we are reminded that Proverbs was written to help the naive (v. 4). In God's world, naivete is not a compliment—it's a condition to change. Verse 5 explains that growing in wisdom is a lifelong project. Counsel from others is a gift from God to help us see what we miss on our own.

Before my daughter's senior year of high school, I asked her to read *She's Got the Wrong Guy*.[5] The author, Deepak Reju, describes ten types of guys that women settle for but should not. Reju speaks from pastoral experience ministering to hundreds of college students and young professionals. I wanted my daughter to gain wisdom from those who have gone before. She did not have personal experience with men like this and therefore needed exposure through the wisdom of someone else. Learning from others encourages, guides, and even warns us about deceptive people.

This concept can be applied to men as well; there are also deceptive and cruel women. Reading through Proverbs, you could come up with your own list of women that no man should want to marry.[6]

Allow those closest to you to offer advice, encouragement, and potential warnings. The next sections will explain why our vision tends to be myopic when we are excited about our relationship.

Our Vision Can Be Clouded by Our Investment

> "For where your treasure is, there your heart will be also." (Matthew 6:21)

Those are powerful words from Jesus. The Bible teaches that our hearts drive our actions and follow our investments. So the heart leads and follows. Relationships take investment as we choose to give our time, mental energy, and money to spend time with others. The more we invest, the more our hearts join the investment. When the other person responds positively, we enjoy the emotions that follow. It seems to me that this explains why some people hang on long after the other person has ended their investment in the relationship.

What have you already invested in your relationship with your boyfriend or girlfriend? Do you spend all of your free time together? That's a big investment. Have you started to dream together about what your future might be like? Have you given the other financial help? Do all your friends see you as a couple? There might be nothing wrong with any of these investments, but if you are more committed to keeping your relationship than you are to wisely assessing it, that could be a problem.

Are there warning signs in your relationship that your boyfriend or girlfriend is not as invested in the relationship as you are? Here are a few examples:

- They do not take the initiative to spend time with you.
- You are always expected to pay for any dinners or entertainment. For many couples, it is reasonable

that the man take the bulk of the commitment, but even men who are happy to pay sometimes wonder if they are being used.

- You alone are being asked to change. Genuine relationships reveal character issues in both people. Thus, if one person does not have growth areas, it probably means they believe they are superior and not in need of change.
- You alone carry the weight of spiritual conversations. Again, we might expect the man to do this, but if she does not reciprocate, then he may need to realize that she is not committed to Jesus.

If you see (or are wondering if you see) these warning signs in your relationship, why don't you ask those who know you best what they see? Your parents, pastors, friends, and mentor might have insight that will be helpful in honestly assessing your relationship. We need those with a more objective assessment, who have not made the same investment, to help us see things that we miss. That is the heart of wisdom explained in Proverbs.

Our Vision Can Be Clouded by the Good Things

Think for a moment about the things you love about your boyfriend or girlfriend, and write them down in the margin. If I could examine your list, it would likely convince me that your boyfriend or girlfriend is awesome. You may have written about their love for the Lord, how they treat you in special ways, the way you see them interact with others, the way they serve without any expectation for return, and the character traits you see in them. This is all good. You should have a list like that.

It is possible, however, that the list has notable omissions. Since we know that perfection cannot be the standard, we may assume that all notable omissions will be filled in later. This is the point where counsel is so important. Will your boyfriend or girlfriend continue to mature? Will they grow in the areas that you are concerned about, or will these become dominant features of their character?

I have no athletic ability, but I liked to compete. This combination often brought out anger in me. I wanted to win, yet no matter how hard I tried, others were better, faster, and stronger. Once, while playing golf, I threw my putter fifty yards toward the next tee because I missed a putt. My actions were childish and sinful. Had Stephanie seen it or known about it, she would have had every right to be concerned. Would I be an angry man who threw things in the house? Would I storm out and leave for three hours because a conversation was not going my way? Would I oppress her and our future children with cruelty and meanness? By God's grace, I did not do those things before marriage or after it, but all too often boyfriends or girlfriends excuse behavior that could be concerning later.

This example also shows that it's important not to judge someone by one bad moment but to look at the trajectory of their life. I wasn't acting right, but God in his grace did help me to see that and change. Look for that kind of response in your significant other when you ask them about an area that is concerning.

Let me tell you about a couple patterns I have observed through my twenty-five years of ministry. First, those who in their thirties or beyond are often quick to excuse their boyfriend's or girlfriend's behavior even amid warnings from family, friends, or pastors. They see the good things. Because they have wanted to be married for a long time, they can view their relationship as their last (or one of their last) opportunities. This encourages them to see what is good and ignore what appear to be clear warnings. Sadly, they not only excuse throwing a putter fifty yards, but they excuse anger directed against them.

Another pattern is being quick to focus on what is true today, rather than carefully evaluating what might be true in the future. I believe that everyone can move beyond their past. Stephen Viars's book, *Putting Your Past in Its Place*,[7] is a biblical theology of dealing with our past. Some are ready to move forward from their past, and others are not. Some are still dominated by past events or patterns. Each of you must remember that five minutes of faithfulness does not necessarily equal a genuine walk with the Lord. Anyone can pretend to be something they are not for a time. Thus, it is helpful to have people in your life who are able to see the good, the bad, and the ugly and have a close enough relationship with you to honestly tell you their thoughts.

Our Vision Can Be Clouded by Our Idolatry

> Their idols are silver and gold, The work of man's hands. They have mouths, but they cannot speak; They have eyes, but they cannot see; They have ears, but they cannot hear; They have noses, but they cannot smell; They have hands, but they cannot feel; They have feet, but they cannot walk; They cannot make a sound with their throat. Those who make them will become like them, Everyone who trusts in them. (Psalm 115:4–8)

We don't like to think of ourselves as idolators, as wanting to glorify and worship anything more than the Lord. But we all struggle with worshiping something or someone who is not God. The intensity of that struggle will determine how much your vision is compromised.

When you read these verses from Psalm 115 about idol worship, you might think that you are off the hook. After all, you don't bow down to a statue. But in this passage, the statue was just a stand-in for Baal, the god the people believed could deliver prosperity. When they bowed down to something that represented a false god, they became like it—dumb, blind, and deaf, unable to smell, feel, or move. The Lord commands his people to trust him instead. It is the only way to see clearly.

What does that have to do with marriage? What happens when a person idolizes being married without submitting their desire for this good thing to God? What happens when a relationship becomes more important than the Lord's honor and glory? You become a person who will not see clearly, one whose vision is clouded. Because your vision can be clouded, it's important to get help from others who might be seeing your relationship more clearly than you can right now.

Encouragement from Family

I know that not everyone grows up in a home that honors the Lord, encourages one another, works together, and confronts one another biblically. Some reading this book may not be able to trust all their parents' advice. But if you have parents who love you and love God, then it's wise to listen to their thoughts about your relationship.

Our grown children do not need our permission to marry, but they would be foolish not to want our blessing. Why? Because we know them. We have experienced great joy as we see them grow into caring adults. We have also experienced the fear and grief that comes from their sinful choices. Like Job, we have served a "priestly" function, interceding for them in ways and times that they did not know. Ask your parents for their advice.

Encouragement from Friends

> Do not forsake your own friend or your father's friend, And do not go to your brother's house in the day of your calamity; Better is a neighbor who is near than a brother far away. (Proverbs 27:10)

There are moments when a friend near is far better than a brother far away. Families may not be in a position to bless your relationship. Maybe a parent has died or struggled with addiction, or refuses to be involved in your life. I grieve for you. You know it should not be that way. If your parents harmed you, then I hope you will seek out help for that issue. But God's grace is so vast that he provides others to love and care for you.

By "friends," I am referring to godly friends who want God's best for you. You don't need their permission to move forward in your relationship, but it would be wise for you to invite them to speak honestly about how they see your relationship. Allow them to say hard things to you about your character and your relationship. The Lord sometimes uses our parents and other times uses a trusted friend to protect us from hardship and redirect us to blessing.

Encouragement from Church Leaders

> Obey your leaders and submit *to them*, for they keep watch over your souls as those who will give an account. Let them do this with joy and not with grief, for this would be unprofitable for you. (Hebrews 13:17)

Did you know that God gives you leaders in the church to watch over you? It's true that some pastors fail at that task, but if your pastor is someone you know and trust, then ask him about your relationship. Would he offer his blessing and celebrate the engagement with you? Perhaps he doesn't know you well enough to answer that question. If not, this is a good time to get to know him and let him get to know you.

What's Your Trajectory?

This chapter emphasizes a growing self-awareness as opposed to self-sufficiency. It encourages you to look for blind spots and genuine concerns you might not see or even want to see. It asks you to humble yourself. Then it emphasizes listening to those who know you best and love you the most. This is a precious gift from the Lord. Not only does Jesus rescue us through his cross, but he places us in his body. Your church was designed to be a protective space for you to learn more about Jesus, to grow in your love for Jesus, and to develop meaningful Christian relationships.

One way to know you are ready for the ring is hearing those who fit that description say that they would celebrate your engagement. There is great joy when the nuclear and church families celebrate God's work in two lives moving toward marriage. If they only tolerate what you have decided, then you increase your risk of having a difficult marriage. The decision is ultimately yours because you will live with the blessings and consequences of your choice, but the wise person thinks carefully about their choices and looks for blessing from others as they move forward.

Reflection Questions

1. Can you identify some ways that your view of your relationship might be clouded? How might others help you get clarity?
2. Read the passages given in the chapter and memorize the one that resonates with you most. Why did you choose that passage?
3. Create a list of people you want to ask about your relationship. This list does not need to be long, but you should also give them several opportunities to see your relationship in different circumstances. For example, have dinner together, go on an adventure together, have a quiet evening together, and so on. Your list could include parents or other close family members, your most trusted friends, and your mentors.

4. Read the story of Saul and Samuel (1 Samuel 9–31). Especially focus on chapters 9–15, 22, 28, and 31 (you can skim the rest). What do you notice about Saul's attitude toward Samuel? What did Saul's commitment to self-sufficiency and self-preservation cost him? Consider whether that should also be a warning to you.
5. If question 3 was hard for you, what relationships do you need to build in order to have people who can speak into your life and relationship?

Chapter 9
Accept Each Other's Life Story

The Big Idea: We marry a person who has a life story we did not write. Rather than attempt to rewrite the story or make the person into something they are not, be honest with them and the Lord. Trust the Lord who writes all our stories, and then decide if you can accept each other's story. If you can, you are one step closer to being ready for the ring.

TWO FRIENDS DECIDED to start dating. One had lost his wife to cancer. The other had divorced her husband for acts of physical violence. They each had children. They were honest with each other. There had to be space for grief, and if they were to move further, they each had to be willing to embrace the life history of the other without jealousy. They would need to figure out holidays and the time spent with each child or grandchild. By God's amazing grace, they both entered with a desire to live for Jesus and allow his Word to dictate their actions. Their love story has been amazing to watch. Their marriage is a testimony of how the Lord can turn mourning into joy.

The Lord writes vivid stories. Each of our lives is a novel full of twists and turns, a beautiful painting on a canvas that only comes together over time. We cannot erase our past. We can move beyond it, but we cannot pretend like it doesn't exist.

We all bring "baggage" into a relationship and marriage. I do not use baggage in a strictly negative way, but as another word to describe our life story.

Sometimes a man or a woman brings with them painful and messy family relationships, prior sexual experiences, overwhelming debt, a child, or a prior broken marriage. As you learn things about your boyfriend's or girlfriend's past, you have a choice. Notice what Jesus says in Luke 14:28:

> "For which one of you, when he wants to build a tower, does not first sit down and calculate the cost to see if he has enough to complete it?"

You can accept them, including the life story that comes with them, or you can decide to end the relationship. If you can't accept all that their life story includes, it's not wrong to end your relationship. It would, however, be wrong to continue pursuing it, despite your misgivings, and then use their past against them for the rest of their lives. What challenges should couples discuss to determine whether they are willing to move forward? Consider these examples.

A Prior Marriage or Child

Some dating couples do not understand the ongoing significance of a prior marriage or child. Some lose a spouse to a devastating illness or accident, but often, it is a result of a failed relationship. Those who have been married before are often more confident in their relational abilities than they should be. If they have not handled their grief, been honest about their failures, realized that a new relationship is not merely replacing the old, and grown in significant ways, then they are prime candidates to struggle in future relationships. They might even sabotage it because they struggle with larger trust issues.

You must decide if you are willing to engage and accept the challenge of being with someone who will be facing their own challenges in moving forward. Their prior relationship might cause you to struggle with your own grief, anger, guilt, or regret. If your boyfriend or girlfriend has been married before, then you must ask yourself whether you are willing to accept that. If you are unwilling, then now is the time to end your relationship.

Some reading this might also hold firm convictions that the only allowable remarriage occurs after the death of a spouse.[8] If that is true for you, then you need to at least pause the relationship to consider what the Bible says. Seek the counsel of a pastor or wise friend. Your thoughts on this might change as you mature and learn more from Scripture and Christ's body. But it is one thing to change as a result of prayer and study and something very different to violate your convictions because you want to marry.[9]

A related concern is a child from a prior relationship. There are many different possible scenarios within this category: the other biological parent might have died or abandoned the child, or both parents might still have a co-parenting relationship. Even under the final category, there can be many different relationship statuses and scenarios.

Let's assume that your boyfriend or girlfriend and the other biological parent work to co-parent. You are the third wheel. This is not necessarily a showstopper, but it is a long-term challenge. There may be tensions between you and the child, you and your future spouse, and you and the other biological parent. You might struggle with being viewed as a second-class parent and not the child's "real mom/dad." You might struggle with grandparents' day because your parents are not invited. You might find the court hearings to discuss custody expensive and irritating. You will most likely have to endure this challenge at least until the child is eighteen years old. Can you accept that your life with your spouse will also include her child (or children) from a previous relationship? Both the child involved and your future spouse deserve to have someone who is all in with them. Are you that person?

Significant Medical Concerns

If your boyfriend or girlfriend has significant medical concerns, now is the time to consider whether you are going to be able to be the support and help that they needs throughout your life together. When you get married, you promise that you are going to be faithful through sickness and health. Of course, you can't know now what your future might hold, but if your present includes medical issues, now is the time to consider if you believe God is calling you to this relationship. There can be great joy in learning to serve someone who is medically fragile, but take some time to think and pray about these issues. If you find yourself in this situation now with your boyfriend or girlfriend, it would be wise to seek counsel from parents, mentors, and pastors. You might also consider talking with a couple who is experiencing physical challenges now so that you can have a sense of what you might face and how you can pray about those things.

Prior Sexual Experience or Other Life-Dominating Sins

What if your boyfriend's or girlfriend's past includes life-dominating sins, even after becoming a Christian? If that's the case, you probably have difficult questions to answer, such as: Have they genuinely repented? Are they different? Can I reasonably trust that they will be faithful to me?

While you must guard against self-righteousness, it is not wrong or unbiblical to question, evaluate, and then determine your next steps. If your boyfriend has used pornography on a regular basis for years, what confidence could you have that he would not return to it after marriage? If your girlfriend has had many sexual partners, what confidence could you have that she would be faithful to you? I realize that these conversations are uncomfortable and hard, but I encourage you to have them now. It only gets harder after engagement.

There are other types of life-dominating sins: anger, bitterness, unwholesome talk, and so on. They can all be clear warning signs that there is a significant problem. Without repentance, cursing after being cut off by a driver could become cursing at your children and calling them harmful names. A propensity to anger could result in a person being violent and physically abusive. Those given to bitterness rather than forgiveness can be very difficult to live with. We all bring immaturity into an engagement. While engagements can be broken, it is far better to address the issues now.

Significant Debt

> The rich rules over the poor, And the borrower *becomes* the lender's slave. (Proverbs 22:7)

College students are in a challenging position. It is very difficult to pay your own expenses for a university education. Wages, especially for entry-level positions, have not risen at the same rate as tuition increases. Although parents can often provide help, the fact remains that many college students graduate with debt. When two people marry, their debts combine. This can be a life-constraining situation.

There are many great jobs that require only technical or vocational training. At the same time, other jobs require a college education. So college tuition can be an investment in the future.

Imagine a scenario where two people who marry each have $30,000 of student loan debt. Once they marry, they now have $60,000. If they each have good-paying jobs and a commitment to pay off their debt as quickly as possible, it is certainly doable. But what happens if only one person has a high-earning potential? It could take years or even decades to clear that debt. It is even worse if both people are not well-versed in money management.

One's financial condition is not the most important aspect of determining readiness for engagement, but how a person thinks about and uses money will either be a source of blessing or a lifelong struggle. If your boyfriend or girlfriend has acquired debt because they believe they are entitled to live how they want, then it is not difficult to see how that attitude toward their finances would be a problem going forward.

Now is a good time to have open conversations and be willing to learn simple money management concepts. For example, you both should know how to create an amortization table. Here is a little test: If you have a $250,000 mortgage at 5% interest for thirty years, then how much would you save and how much time would you take off the loan if you paid an extra $100 per month? Does each person know the rule of 72? Are you each committed to using a budget and following it faithfully, meaning you don't go over budget and the budget doesn't change without discussion between the two of you?[10]

What's Your Trajectory?

This chapter comes from my years in ministry working with struggling couples. Many of their problems were evident while they dated, but neither had the courage to address those issues before they married. That opened the door to significant struggles in their relationship that often centered around the issues raised in this chapter. So please take these items seriously and speak openly with your boyfriend or girlfriend. Ask the Lord to help you both change, grow, and mature so that you are ready to enter marriage joyfully, able to embrace all that the Lord has for you as a couple.

The Lord writes wonderful stories. The older we get, the more we can look back at the Lord's work and marvel at what he did. I am convinced that your life will be a beautiful picture of his grace. But marriage is a choice. We decide who to marry, and when we do, we must accept them for who they are. While they still need to change, grow, and mature, we promise to help them bear any burden, rejoice in victory, grieve loss, and overcome prior decisions. This is a high, wonderful, and serious calling.

My wife and I had the joy of entering marriage with our life stories and past experiences but without long-term responsibilities. This allowed us to embrace the new joys and challenges of marriage on their own terms. It was impossible to know all that the Lord would do with us and what we would experience, but it was a true joy to have eyes focused on our future rather than caught in our past. Whatever your life story and the challenges you bring into a relationship, I want that same joy for you.

Reflection Questions

1. Make a list of items in your past that have significant present consequences. Discuss them with your mentor.
2. Talk with your boyfriend or girlfriend and your mentor and determine what items might be relationship stoppers, what can be handled together, and what should be handled through a separate individual process. Be honest with each other.
3. Commit that if you decide to move forward, you will follow the plan to address the items and only speak about them in a productive way (solution-oriented rather than problem-centered).
4. When you are ready, talk about ways you can limit temptation and encourage faithfulness moving forward. For example, if one of you has struggled with financial responsibilities, what safeguards will you put in place to ensure that person does not travel the same path?

Chapter 10
Guard Against Social Media

The Big Idea: Social media has changed how people interact with the world. Some of this change is beneficial. However, social media, and those who are loosely connected to us through it, can be given inappropriate influence in our decision-making.

WHEN MY WIFE and I married in 1993, we did not have an online profile, a cell phone, or a car phone. We had never even heard the term "social media." Those were simpler times! Your story is likely different. You might have met through a dating app, posted pictures together on your respective social media accounts, and received many comments and likes. It is part of the way that you do life. Since that is true, I would like you to consider some of the blessings and possible challenges of social media and how it may have shaped your relationship.

The Blessings of Social Media

Let's start with three blessings. First, social media allows others to be excited about your relationship. Dating is exciting. It feels good to be loved, and we want others to celebrate with us when our dreams come true. Social media gives us that opportunity. When people engage with, comment on, or like a post of you and your boyfriend or girlfriend doing something fun, it feels good. It makes you feel special. There is something wonderful and encouraging about it.

Second, social media gives you a voice among those who follow you. Many prominent Christians are active on social media. They believe it is one way to reach people with gospel content. You might be doing an amazing job using your social media content to encourage others' faith in Jesus, strengthen the church, and evangelize the lost. It is possible that your relationship with your boyfriend or girlfriend provides even more opportunities to proclaim Jesus and the truth of his Word. If so, great job! The Lord is pleased by your boldness to use your platform to advance the cause of Christ.

Third, social media allows you to learn about creative ideas for showing love and encouraging your boyfriend or girlfriend. As your friends and those you follow post exciting moments of their lives, you can get ideas for date nights, engagement plans, and other ways to care for your significant other. These resources were not as easily available in the days prior to social media.

Rather than discredit social media entirely, I believe it can be used to share your excitement, glorify the Lord, and learn creative ways to love and care for your boyfriend or girlfriend. When my wife and I dated, became engaged, and got married, few knew about our relationship because we lived during a time where phones were attached to the wall, phone books were delivered yearly, and news spread through word of mouth. We did not have the opportunity to learn from or reach a wider audience.

The Challenges of Social Media

Social media, however, can also be destructive. Without wisdom and maturity, it often does more harm than good. That is why the way you handle social media is an important aspect of determining whether you're ready for the ring. Consider the following three dangers.

Unhelpful influence

Social media can have an unhelpful influence on the way you think about relationships in general and your significant other in particular. My twenty-two-year-old son has helped me understand some of the major differences between my day and his and how the world of dating has changed. Now, people who may have no active part in your life have immediate access via social media. Information flows in both directions since you also have access to their life. This highway of information and easy access complicates the dating horizon in two ways.

First, social media magnifies a young person's fear of man. There is pressure to download and use various social media apps to communicate, share, and create community with peers. While social media can be helpful in this regard, it also provides a platform for unhelpful ideas in your relationship. For example, trends focusing on "know your worth" and slogans like "as he/she should" are unhelpful as they often focus on superficial, worldly ideas and expectations.

Second, social media provides easy opportunities for comparison and covetousness. Scrolling provides opportunity to compare someone else's best day with your worst. For example, it is difficult to see a post of a couple from church smiling and happy right after you had a rough conversation with your boyfriend or girlfriend. This comparison is dangerous and unhelpful when seeking to grow in a relationship with Christ at the center.

Unbiblical relationship guides

Friends, followers, or so-called "relationship experts" can become your primary source of information about how to manage your relationship. Taking our first point one step further, your friends or followers might take the next step of giving you advice on how to manage your relationship. Even more likely, what you read online from influencers or self-help accounts might become your source of relationship advice. Remember to be careful of any advice that does not come from a biblical worldview.

Resist the danger of allowing someone who doesn't know you well to have influence over your relationship decisions (or any decisions!). It's fine to have online friends and followers, but do not give them a voice into your dating relationship unless they are involved in your life and have the spiritual maturity to say something worth hearing.

I am not suggesting that you use social media only to post and that you reject all conversations. But I do suggest that you need the maturity to know when you must ignore the comments of others.

Harmful use of information

I wish this was not true, but social media can be dangerous. One of my friends is a detective. He investigates extortion crimes against children and young adults. He says that social media has provided a tool that evil people use to harm others. They pretend to be a friend or follower and look for weaknesses and opportunities. This may sound extreme, but pictures of you and your boyfriend or girlfriend provide information and opportunities for evil people to harm you. Some AI systems can "create" additional pictures of you from a real image. It is difficult to say how they might be used in the future. Cyberbullying is a real problem. Social media allows almost anyone to attack areas of your vulnerability. Wise is the couple who understands these dangers and makes appropriate decisions based on these facts.

Wise Ways to Navigate Social Media

Some people opt to eliminate their digital exposure, but if that is not the option you choose, here are a few pieces of advice to consider.

First, intentionally post to make a difference for Christ. Consider 1 Peter 2:9–10:

> But you are A CHOSEN RACE, A royal PRIESTHOOD, A HOLY NATION, A PEOPLE FOR *God's* OWN POSSESSION, so that you may proclaim the excellencies of Him who has called you out of darkness into His marvelous light; for you once were NOT A PEOPLE, but now you are THE PEOPLE OF GOD; you had NOT RECEIVED MERCY, but now you have RECEIVED MERCY.

Social media allows us to communicate any message at any time. The more you are motivated by your desire to share Christ, the less you are concerned about yourself. The picture of you at dinner, on a walk, or on a roller coaster is not nearly as important as words where you share about the Lord's blessings. This also tends to create more reaction from those who have a similar desire, which helps to create a community where Christ is central. This larger social community then serves as a protection against those who might want to harm you. Social media uses its own algorithm to deliver content to you and to push your content to others. That creates a "community" for you. The more you post about dinners, walks, and roller coasters, the more you will connect to others who like those things too. When you post about Jesus, that creates a community of Jesus people.

Second, ignore unsolicited comments or messages from those who don't know you. Our friends and followers, as well as those who find us through the community created by social media's algorithm, may choose to comment or send a direct message that is negative or seeking to give advice on your relationship. My encouragement is to ignore all of it. Your parents, family, close friends, mentors, and church family talk to you personally. They are the ones in the best position to give you wise advice. As Proverbs 18:13 says, "He who gives an answer before he hears, It is folly and shame to him." Social media allows for anyone to react. People make judgments based on the few facts they see online. However, if they have not been part of your relationship, seen you and your boyfriend or girlfriend interact, or understood your stress points or why you are interested in one another, then their judgments are superficial.

Finally, be careful what you post. Since social media can be used for good or evil, avoid providing compromising information. We cannot prevent people from harming us if that is their desire, but we can avoid providing them with ammunition.

What's Your Trajectory?

You may be using social media for God's glory. You may know how to post, who to DM, and how to ignore those who have nothing to contribute. However, if your social media use is more problematic than a blessing, then this is a good time to discuss with your mentor your social media use and how to use it for God's glory. The Lord is so gracious. Not only has he provided his Word, but he has put you in the body of Christ and given you the Holy Spirit to help you discern good from evil. The more you trust the Lord's voice and the voice of his mature people who love you, the more you will be able to use your social media for joy and have the discernment to ignore the negative, harmful, and foolish.

Reflection Questions

1. How do you use social media? Have you defined the type of content you want to post and the type you should not?
2. Why do you look at others' social media pages? Are you killing time, looking for escape from reality, or engaging with purpose?
3. Share with your boyfriend or girlfriend your experience with social media and ask them about their experience. What themes do you notice?
4. Review your posts from the last few months. Is there anything you wish you did not include? What would you have done differently (not said anything, changed your wording, etc.)?
5. What steps would you take if you or your boyfriend or girlfriend experienced cyberbullying?

Chapter 11
Be Willing to Accept More Responsibility

> **The Big Idea:** Engagement is a big and exciting step. Before you take that step, take some time to consider what responsibilities come with marriage that you don't have as a single person. Before you propose or say yes, consider a few commitments implied when you enter a marriage covenant before the Lord and your invited guests.

DURING MY COLLEGE freshman orientation, someone gave me a piece of paper inviting me to join the rowing club. I had never heard of rowing, but I thought it might be fun. Over a hundred attended the first callout meeting. Since that was far more than they could coach and train, the first five days were torture. We did not touch a boat or an oar. We were on land doing countless runs, sprints, jumping jacks, burpees, and push-ups. The coaches wanted to find out who actually wanted to be there. This chapter serves as a kind of gut check. You owe it to the Lord and to your potential spouse to be willing to accept the responsibilities associated with marriage.

After your wedding, you will both learn many truths about each other, about marriage, and about how two people live together for Jesus. By God's grace, all you learn will help you enjoy your marriage and family. But now is a good time to think about the Lord's expectations for husbands and wives.

Expectation #1: Husbands Learn and Show Honor and Wives Focus on Character and Submit

> In the same way, you wives, be submissive to your own husbands so that even if any of *them* are disobedient to the word, they may be won without a word by the behavior of their wives, as they observe your chaste and respectful behavior. Your adornment must not be *merely* external—braiding the hair, and wearing gold jewelry, or putting on dresses; but *let it be* the hidden person of the heart, with the imperishable quality of a gentle and quiet spirit, which is precious in the sight of God. For in this way in former times the holy women also, who hoped in God, used to adorn themselves, being submissive to their own husbands; just as Sarah obeyed Abraham, calling him lord, and you have become her children if you do what is right without being frightened by any fear. You husbands in the same way, live with your *wives* in an understanding way, as with someone weaker, since she is a woman; and show her honor as a fellow heir of the grace of life, so that your prayers will not be hindered. (1 Peter 3:1–7)

The Bible teaches that both husbands and wives have responsibilities in marriage that neither has during dating or engagement. Of course, the Scripture passages describing marital roles are not the only texts that address marriage. There are many passages related to worshiping and making the Lord the center of our lives, our character, our goals and the way we communicate. Every one of those passages will affect the kind of marriage we enjoy.

This chapter presents those texts that address the specific responsibilities of husbands and wives in marriage. Men are not required to live with all women according to knowledge or show them honor. Nor are women required to respect and submit to all men. The Lord has high expectations for those who take on the extra responsibility of marriage.

For men: Learn to understand

This command could involve simple matters like knowing her favorite restaurant, color, or clothing store, but it also involves so much more. When a man signs up for this responsibility, he knows that understanding his wife involves knowing her fears, the things that give her joy, ways that he scares her or protects her, ways that she feels special, and ways that confirm in her heart that she made a good decision in marrying him.

In the previous chapter, you thought about your significant other's life story and how that story might affect her response to different events. Part of living with her in an understanding way involves finding ways to bring her life.

During a church leadership training day, our facilitator encouraged each of us to do one life-giving task per day. He reminded us that sometimes ministry is hard and it helps to practice this each day. This can be a helpful application for marriage. Men, when you eventually live with your wife, that includes finding opportunities to give her life. That might be a little challenging to do right now while you are dating. However, learning to send a kind note, taking a favorite drink to her workplace, or giving her any other reminder that you listen to her and care for her is a sign that you are ready for the next step.

Living with your wife according to knowledge requires effort. It is not fair to expect a twenty-three-year-old to understand, lead, or show honor like a seasoned veteran. Remember, this entire book is focused on trajectory, not perfection. But husbands, no matter what their age or maturity level, should be willing to do what God has called them to do in marriage. And it's also important to be humble enough to know when you need help.

For men: Show honor

When you are married, God calls you to see your wife as a recipient of God's grace who ultimately belongs to him, not you. Prior to our sons' respective marriages, we hoped they would be husbands that honored their wives. We hoped that the example they saw growing up would be the lowest standard they hoped to achieve. We wanted the women who married our sons to receive blessing and honor from them. In the same way, we trust that the Lord will provide a man for our daughter who cares for her, who remembers that she is not his possession but God's, and who treats her with honor.

Remember that your wife is called to a role that is not always easy. Her responsibilities described below place her in a position of weakness. It is crucial that you care well for her.

How might you, as a boyfriend, show her honor? First, you show honor in the way you speak to and about your girlfriend. Years ago, I worked at a job where many men referred to their wives as their "ol' lady." They also often complained about the state of their marriage. That's the opposite of showing honor!

Second, you show her honor in the way you handle her weaknesses. God gifted all of us with certain strengths and weaknesses. You honor another person when you encourage them, help them, or protect them. You can't take a test for another person, but you can help them study and exercise patience when they ask you for help again and again.

Third, you show honor by not taking what does not belong to you. Some boyfriends push their girlfriends to have sex with them or challenge the limits. Self-centeredness and manipulation demands, but honor waits and shows consideration.

For women: Focus on character

Every society has a standard of beauty. With so much exposure through TV, news, and social media, women face consistent pressure to meet a standard of beauty that they see portrayed in our culture. So it is not hard to understand how some women get caught in unhealthy eating, overexercise, and an inordinate focus on their appearance.

Your heavenly Father wants to free you from this pressure. He wants you to focus on your character. He wants you to be known as a woman who knows how to love the Lord above all, to be motivated by his saving grace, and to be guided every day by his Word. The life of faith in Jesus is where we daily walk with him, learn about him, pray without ceasing, lament our pain, trust in our waiting, and grow in our love for God and others.

As you follow Jesus, ask the Spirit to help you spend more time in God's Word and in caring for others than you spend on your eating habits or your exercise routine. Protect your time with Jesus, your serving, and your attendance in your local church. Learn to speak with others about your struggles.

For women: Learn to submit

No woman is called to submit to her boyfriend during dating or engagement as she would her husband when married. Until you stand together before the Lord and your witnesses and enter the marriage covenant, you are not required to submit. But since this is a part of being married, you can provide a few tests during your dating period. Decide, of your own free will, to submit to something your boyfriend requests. Did his request move you toward the Lord? For example, he asked you to join a Bible study he attends on Thursday evening. You don't really want your Thursday evenings tied up, but you decide to give yourself some practice. How did it go? Are you concerned about how your boyfriend will handle this responsibility when you are married? Will he call you to follow him as he follows Christ? And are you concerned about your willingness to follow? These are good questions to ask right now.

Expectation #2: Husbands Love and Wives Respect

> Wives, *be subject* to your own husbands, as to the Lord. For the husband is the head of the wife, as Christ also is the head of the church, He Himself *being* the Savior of the body. But as the church is subject to Christ, so also the wives *ought to be* to their husbands in everything. Husbands, love your wives, just as Christ also loved the church and gave Himself up for her, so that He might sanctify her, having cleansed her by the washing of water with the word, that He might present to Himself the church in all her glory, having no spot or wrinkle or any such thing; but that she would be holy and blameless. So husbands ought also to love their own wives as their own bodies. He who loves his own wife loves himself; for no one ever hated his own flesh, but nourishes and cherishes it, just as Christ also *does* the church, because we are members of His body. FOR THIS REASON A MAN SHALL LEAVE HIS FATHER AND MOTHER AND SHALL BE JOINED TO HIS WIFE, AND THE TWO SHALL BECOME ONE FLESH. This mystery is great; but I am speaking with reference to Christ and the church. Nevertheless, each individual among you also is to love his own wife even as himself, and the wife must *see to it* that she respects her husband. (Ephesians 5:22–33)

For men: Love your wives as Christ loves the church

This passage sets the bar high for any man considering a ring. Admittedly, no husband lives up to it. But there is a significant difference between a man who does not even try to love his wife like this and the man who believes Christ's love for the church is the gold standard and works to achieve it. We come back to trajectory versus perfection. To the men reading this book, your willingness to move toward Christlike love is an important factor of whether you are ready for the ring. Here are a few questions you can ask yourself to determine the quality of your love:

- Who sacrifices more to be together?
- Looking at your previous five dates, how much planning did she do?
- How have you responded when she expressed worry about something (a test, a job situation, seeing a particular person, etc.)? Did you support her (help her study, give advice for her job, go with her to see the person, etc.)?
- How have you been gentle with her heart? Have you been clear with your intentions, or has she spent time guessing?
- How have you celebrated her successes and proven that she can succeed without being jealous of her?

Some men use the impossible standard of Christ's love for the church as an excuse not to love. Godly men ready to buy a ring and start preparing for marriage are on the trajectory of learning to love like Jesus does. They are submitting to the Lord's instructions, finding ways to live it out practically, and repenting when they don't live up to God's standard of love.

For women: Respect your husbands

I have often met with husbands who struggle with the feeling that their wives do not value them. This is hard for men. Sometimes the men are overdramatic, but other times they are speaking the truth. Some men live with women who put them down, complain about the kind of work they do, and criticize how they parent.

There is a better way. If your boyfriend is not a man who loves Jesus, cares for others, and is deserving of respect, then it is best to end the relationship. However, if your boyfriend loves Jesus with his whole heart, is growing in his love for you, and works diligently for the Lord (whether in his studies, at his job, or while serving in a local church ministry), then respecting, valuing, and appreciating him should be your goal.

If you are concerned about his ability to financially provide, then please talk about it. Jobs are paid by market value, not biblical value. Biblically, every job is meaningful. Those who stock shelves at the local grocery store are not paid above the national average, but the job they do is valuable—especially when you go to the store looking for something no one bothered to put on the shelf! If you decide you are ready for engagement, then you are deciding that his job's level of provision is worthy of respect and appreciation.

What's Your Trajectory?

As this stage in your relationship, you should not completely fulfill the husband/wife roles. You are independent from each other. However, you should be willing to put your toe in the water. Women, practice appreciation, willingly submit to something to see how it goes, and focus on developing godly character. Guys, learn about what's really important to your girlfriend. Sometimes she will appreciate ice cream and a walk in the park accompanied by questions that get to her heart more than a fancy date. Be the one who sacrifices so that it is clear to her that you are pursuing her rather than settling. Celebrate her successes, and remember that she belongs to Jesus. If you both are moving in these directions, you have good reason to believe you are ready for the ring.

If you have identified struggles in your life or the life of your significant other, then all hope is not lost. It indicates that you need to grow in your love and appreciation for Jesus. As you reflect on how Christ saves, loves, encourages, helps, and provides for you, your capacity for loving others will increase.

It is sometimes amazing to see how much the Lord changes our willingness to submit to his Word through understanding his great love for us.

Reflection Questions

1. Talk together about the examples of godly marriages you have seen, such as parents, friends, coworkers, or couples from church. Set up a meeting to talk to two couples and ask them how they practice 1 Peter 3:1–7 and Ephesians 5:22–33.
2. Each of you create a list of the ways you are living out these passages now. Compare your lists and discuss the differences.
3. Identify the portion of the passages that you believe will be most difficult to fulfill and why that is true for you. (For example, maybe you are competitive and like to win. This means others must lose, which could make showing honor to your girlfriend/wife difficult.)
4. Create a list of three ways you can start applying these verses to your relationship.
5. Discuss with your mentor what they observe about you personally and as part of a couple. What trajectory are you on?

Conclusion
Trust in the Lord with All Your Heart

Trust in the Lord with all your heart
And do not lean on your own understanding.
In all your ways acknowledge Him,
And He will make your paths straight.
(PROVERBS 3:5–6)

For I am confident of this very thing, that He who began a good work in you will perfect it until the day of Christ Jesus.
(PHILIPPIANS 1:6)

IF YOU MADE it this far—congratulations! You are taking your relationships with God and with your boyfriend or girlfriend seriously. Now, as you consider whether or not you are ready for the ring, remember that you can't know everything. You can't know for sure what the ongoing character of your boyfriend or girlfriend will be over the next several decades. You also can't know all that the Lord will allow in your lives until he takes you home. Being completely sure and setting a perfectionistic standard for yourself or your boyfriend or girlfriend were never the goals of working through this material.

It is also true that there are many who would have never read a book like this and have done just fine. My father decided to marry my mom the day they met. They met, dated, and got married in rapid speed. They dated all wrong! But in God's grace, he took two unbelievers committed to each other, saved them, and grew them. My parents have been married fifty-six years, and I have never once seen them in a heated argument. God did an amazing work, and there are many such examples. But it is also true that there were many others who did things my parent's way and have had fifty-six years of division, strife, brokenness, and perhaps divorce. So I am thankful that you thought something like this book would be helpful.

You decided to read this book to help you answer the question of whether you are ready for the ring. You studied and answered questions to discern the wisdom of moving forward. Remember that moving forward, waiting, and ending the relationship are all possible good outcomes. I trust that the Lord is providing clarity for your next steps in your relationship. I hope that you pursue those steps with joy, even if your decision might be painful.

Although you can't know everything for sure, there are some things you can be sure of: You can be sure that if you trust the Lord with all your heart, he will lead you. You can be sure that the Lord will use your current relationship, or your desire for one, to mold you into the man or woman that he wants you to be. You can be sure that the Lord will be at work in you all the way until the day of Christ.

May the Lord richly bless you as you seek to live faithfully for him.

A Note to Parents and Mentors

THANK YOU, PARENTS and mentors, for being willing to engage with this material. I realize it is a sacrifice of your limited time, energy, and resources. I have a few thoughts specifically for parents, and then I will provide some guidance for those using this material as mentors.

To Parents

I mentioned in the introduction that my personal circumstances motivated me to write this book. In the past few years, both of our sons became engaged and married delightful young women. We had many talks about life, the Lord, girls, and how to discern whether you truly have a life partner. Our daughter is now in college thinking through her relationships. Thus, I find myself reviewing these same concepts with her. I hope this resource helps and encourages you as you build adult relationships with your adult children. I have four final pieces of advice before I close. This advice is one parent speaking to another. Take it for what it is worth.

Communicate often your support of your child and your desire for God's best

> Then the LORD spoke to Moses, saying, "Speak to Aaron and to his sons, saying, 'Thus you shall bless the sons of

> Israel. You shall say to them: The LORD bless you, and keep you; The LORD make His face shine on you, And be gracious to you; The LORD lift up His countenance on you, And give you peace.'" (Numbers 6:22–26)

When I started the dating/engagement/marriage journey with my children, I thought I should approve of my child's choice for a spouse. Without realizing it, I created a barrier for my children to cross—dad's approval. This led them to be less open out of fear that I would be disappointed. I realized I needed to change. If I placed "my approval" at the center of their dating relationships, then everyone would lose. They would lose because they might overlook true issues in the relationship. I would lose the chance to influence them, and others (like their future children) might lose if they made poorly motivated decisions now. My pride needed to be exchanged for something far better.

I knew that abdicating my role as their father could not possibly be right either. The Lord gave me the privilege of being their father, and I needed to be a godly one. Psalm 127 and 128 extol the blessings of children. We were living proof of it. However, instead of being proud or placing obstacles on them, I needed to think about how *I could bless them*. That is what I wanted anyway. The Bible has numerous instances of fathers blessing their children (Jacob and Joseph, to name just two). I wanted my boys (now men) to marry wonderful women and for them to enjoy whatever the Lord has planned for them—that is, to be blessed. Now, I want my daughter to have a godly man who will love, learn from, lead, cherish, and treasure her. This means, among other things, that I needed to find ways to bless and support everything that was right about their choices.

Once they believed that I was on their team rather than a boss who needed to be appeased, they could speak openly with me. We could celebrate together the good moments and talk meaningfully about items of concern. Once they knew I supported them and wanted God's very best for them, our common goal allowed for free communication in both directions. By God's amazing grace, we have been able to give our full and unrestrained blessing to our boys and their wives.

As your children age, you want them to believe that you *want* to bless them. If they do, they will not only give you influence, but they are far more likely to want an ongoing relationship with you. Should your child marry, then their spouse is also more inclined to want to be with you because you consider them a blessing. The Lord in his grace has kept our children close in proximity to us. Every Sunday night we have a family dinner that includes all five of our children coming to enjoy a meal and fellowship with us. Blessing their relationships has resulted in us reaping a greater blessing.

Be an intercessor for your children

> There was a man in the land of Uz whose name was Job; and that man was blameless, upright, fearing God and turning away from evil. Seven sons and three daughters were born to him. His possessions also were 7,000 sheep, 3,000 camels, 500 yoke of oxen, 500 female donkeys, and very many servants; and that man was the greatest of all the men of the east. His sons used to go and hold a feast in the house of each one on his day, and they would send and invite their three sisters to eat and drink with them. When the days of feasting had completed their cycle, Job would send and consecrate them, rising up early in the morning and offering burnt offerings *according to* the number of them all; for Job said, "Perhaps my sons have sinned and cursed God in their hearts." Thus Job did continually. (Job 1:1–5)

This passage is inspirational. I don't remember when I first learned it, but I remember reading it differently when I became a dad. I wanted our children to live righteously for Jesus. As my children grew, I learned that I had far less control over their choices. Then, as they grew older, my days of offering formal discipline for their decisions ended. Although my ability to control my children changed, I could still go to the Lord. I did not know all that my children were doing. I am sure there was a protective grace in that. But apparently Job did not know everything his children were doing either. With Job, I could always go to Jesus and ask, "Lord, if my children have dishonored you tonight, please forgive them and restore them to a right relationship with you." That prayer never gets old. It will help you remember that your children belong to the Lord and they have their own relationship with Jesus to build.

I also needed to pray for my wife and myself. The Lord loves your children more than you do. I needed to tell myself that. The Lord has a plan for their life that might be different from your plan. Again, I needed to tell myself that, especially if I thought their choices were moving them away from the Lord. The Lord's work does not end until the day of Christ. Although I could not see the whole picture, I had to believe that God would continue his work in them, just as he was doing in me. I needed to pray that I would not be a barrier and repent over my heart attitudes. The same was true for my wife. She shared my concerns and of course had additional ones. We needed to encourage each other as we watched our children leave our nest and make choices for themselves.

I am not necessarily suggesting that you tell them how often you pray Job 1:5 for them. We do not want to give our children the impression that we are assuming they will be foolish. However, I believe you can tell them that you pray for this, while also explaining some of your other prayer requests. Our children are helped by knowing that their parents intercede to Jesus for them.

Be courageous

> "Have I not commanded you? Be strong and courageous! Do not tremble or be dismayed, for the LORD your God is with you wherever you go." (Joshua 1:9)

This passage is the Lord's commission to Joshua amid a tremendously difficult responsibility. Parenting is also a difficult responsibility that only gets harder as children grow older. As a young dad, I didn't know that (thankfully!). But now I realize that the sleepless nights with an infant, the temper tantrums with a toddler, and the drama of junior high were there to prepare us parents for the real battles. My first two pieces of advice caution us from being too prideful, authoritarian, or too aggressive with them (we just talk to Jesus instead). But sometimes you do need to say something.

Let's imagine that you are concerned about your child's dating choice. You want to say something, but you are not sure you should or even how to say it. You understand that you are in a risky situation. If you say something your child doesn't like, they might shut you out. You might not have a good future relationship with their spouse should your child push forward anyway. Wisdom, love, and blessing might encourage you to wait, to let things play out, to watch and see if your initial judgments were hasty and wrong. During this waiting period, you pray and intercede.

But then, it is possible that now you have all the information you need. You, unlike your child, are not blinded by an emotional attachment, a desire for a spouse, or the envy of others. You see it for what it is—an impending disaster. Parent, I know what you are thinking and feeling. I have been there too.

Now might be a time to take the risk and exercise great courage and strength. You might need to be strong, be courageous, and choose righteousness over fear. If you say nothing, you could miss the chance to help your child avoid a bad choice. These choices can bring a lot of pain, suffering, and hardship for them and for others for years to come. A poor marriage decision can radically change their life and might change yours too.

I encourage you to think, pray, and potentially seek pastoral advice before lowering a major boom. We want to use our parental position and authority wisely. Sometimes we wait, keep praying and talking, but other times we must courageously appeal to our child even though we might be risking future relationships. Why would you do that? Only because that would please Jesus and might rescue your child from a poor decision. Who knows—maybe the Lord will allow that conversation to be powerful and meaningful. Besides, if you do not have godly strength, courage, and commitment when it comes to your child, who will?

We ask the Lord for wisdom, and then we do our best to communicate with encouragement, affirming our love and support. Let me share an illustration. One of our children went away to college and met a girl he seemed to like. He wanted to bring her home to meet us. We were more than happy to accommodate his request. In fact, we planned a few special "dates" for our family to spend time with her and set aside some extra money to make it special. During her visit, our family was shocked by her behavior. We could not believe the contempt in the way she treated our son and our efforts to engage with her.

At the end of the week, I had to risk it. I knew my relationship with my son was a little tense, but I believed I had no choice. I told him that his mother and I loved him and we would do everything in our power to love whoever he married. We would, for our part, consider her our daughter too.

However, after experiencing the previous five days with his girlfriend, I told him he should end the relationship because of the things we had seen when she visited. Thankfully, he followed our advice and ended the relationship. In God's amazing grace, we enjoy a great relationship today, and the Lord provided him with a woman who is far more precious than gold.

I realize God blessed this moment. It could have gone differently. Our concern could have negatively defined our relationship forever. In this case, I did not think I had a choice. Appeal to him or sit and watch him ruin his life—that was my choice. Parents, it is hard to be courageous. I understand! We need great wisdom to know when to speak and when to remain quiet. But if you think your son or daughter is about to be run over by a train, the loving thing to do is warn them to get off the track.

Encourage outside counsel

> Without consultation, plans are frustrated, But with many counselors they succeed. (Proverbs 15:22)

Parents, encourage your children to be around other godly people who can influence them. We are to disciple and train our children. Shame on us if we abdicate that responsibility. But that does not mean we must do so alone. We take responsibility, but we also bring as many resources to help us as possible. Parents are first responsible to educate their children. Some parents teach their children math, physics, chemistry, logic, and writing. But most of us, even homeschooling parents, get help from curriculum or online teaching resources that allow us to help our children in ways for which we are not fully equipped. You bring your children to Sunday school and youth group where others will teach them the Bible. That does not mean parents do not pray with their children, teach them the Bible, or help them understand how the Bible should direct their actions.

As your children reach dating and engagement age, continue to look for people who will encourage their faith. If your children are at college, then encourage them to seek out mentors that will also speak into whether or not they are ready for the ring. Our grown children will be the ones who must initiate and allow others to have a voice, but we should be encouraging them and even helping them to find godly mentors. The more godly people your children have around them, the better.

To Mentors

Thank you for being willing to lead others through this material. When I lead people through it, I use a threefold strategy. First, I briefly explain the section I want them to read. For example, if we are ready for chapter 3, "Be United in Purpose, Convictions, and Direction," I explain how God has designed all of us to function in certain ways in his body. As we read the Word, we develop convictions. The clearer our purpose and convictions, the clearer our direction. Both the young man and the young woman need to ask whether the Lord has called them to move in the same direction. This summary ensures that they know the basic content before they read it. This summary is in "The Big Idea" section that starts each chapter.

Second, I ask them to read the chapter, write out answers individually to the reflection questions at the end, and then discuss their answers together. Writing tends to produce more thoughtful answers.

Third, I go over the material and review their answers. I do not normally cover all the questions. I may decide to ask different questions that are tailored to their situation. The longer I meet with them and the more I learn, the more specific I can be.

What am I looking for? I think it is best to have a target. Maybe it helps to describe the target we want as well as the target we might get.

Discern if they have a learner's heart and willingly make specific changes

I love to see people respond to the Word with a learner's heart, making specific changes in how they function. When you see them both allowing the Word—instead of culture or comfort—to determine their choices, then you all can rejoice. You should also see them both either drawing closer together or realizing that their relationship cannot move forward. This may sound surprising. As they draw closer to the Lord, they might discover that the Lord has them moving in opposite directions. Their appreciation and love for one another grows as they become more Christlike, but so does their conviction that love for the other means letting them go to run in the direction the Lord wants and find another person taking that same path.

Clarity for both of them is the best outcome. That is the target. In this case, you are there to lead, guide, redirect, and encourage. You may not need to share your opinions because the Lord makes it clear to the couple. They either move joyfully to engagement, or they move apart with joy (and possibly grief as well), allowing each to pursue Christ wholeheartedly.

Respond to a resistant heart

It is possible that instead of seeing humble people who desire to be more like Jesus, you see resistance, immaturity, and blame-shifting. There are a few possible outcomes. First, one person's resistance may be so obvious that their boyfriend or girlfriend ends the relationship. Praise the Lord. Ending a relationship is a reasonable outcome for this study. It is easy to put on a show for a while. However, people's true character and commitment to Jesus come out when pressed.

Second, it is possible that both are resistant, or that one is resistant and the other does not seem bothered by it. This makes your mentoring more challenging. Read the previous section to parents for reminders to pray and decide when to exercise patience or courage.

I believe that the Lord is sovereign in our attempts to help others. That means I can focus on what the Lord wants me to do without bearing the full weight of others' decisions. I have officiated a wedding or two where I seriously wondered if it would last. I encouraged, exhorted, warned, and prayed. I decided not to make a scene by refusing to participate. But I communicated clearly and expressed my honest concerns. At that point, I gave it up to the Lord, trusting that what I did honored him. I, like many who are willing to get involved in personal ministry, have been blamed for not doing this or doing too much of that. Maybe I deserved those criticisms, or maybe they were exhibiting the same kind of immaturity and blame-shifting I warned them about, and they were looking for some place to put their guilt.

Remember as you try to help this couple that you are not the Lord. Sometimes it is helpful to remember that we are tools in the hands of our Redeemer; we are not the Redeemer. Thank you for being willing to be an instrument in his hand. Learn the lessons every case has to offer, but also remember that you are responsible to serve the Lord. The couple must still make decisions and accept the blessings and consequences that come from their choices.

Understand your role

There will be times when a couple reaches a clear conclusion because of your counsel. You hope for that. You want their hearts exposed, and you want them to make a wise decision based on what they learn. It is possible, however, that they will want you to tell them what to do. Just because they ask does not necessarily mean you must answer.

I do not believe mentors have authority in these decisions. One might even argue that parents do not, depending upon the circumstances. The people we serve come freely and can choose to end the mentoring at any time. Thus, it is helpful to remember that you are there to advise, encourage, and assist. Our goal is to help them think, pray, learn, and decide. We cannot possibly know everything they will face or how they will respond in the future. Thus, I prefer to tell them the positive things I have seen and my areas of concern. I might even recommend future steps. However, I am there to encourage and guide, not to determine their next steps.

May the Lord give you the grace and strength to lead wisely and encourage couples to live more faithfully for Jesus.

Acknowledgments

AS I LOOK back over my fifty-four years of life, I cannot believe the journey the Lord has taken me on. Saving me at an early age, moving our family to a new church at just the right time, discipling me through my pastor, calling me out of my first career and into ministry, and then giving me the chance to impact people with the truth of the gospel. Jesus has done so much. It is honestly difficult to comprehend it. This book, I hope, brings him honor and glory. I hope my words, in both content and tone, please him. Psalm 19:14 is my prayer—"May the words of my mouth and the meditation of my heart Be acceptable in Your sight, O Lord, my rock and my Redeemer."

I want to thank Faith Church, its leadership and members, for their constant encouragement to learn and then encourage others. Thank you! It has been a joy to serve for the last twenty years and to look forward to the years still to come.

My wife and life partner, Stephanie, has also encouraged me far beyond what I deserve. Her constant support and care gave me the freedom to think, work, and invest in another writing project. I also appreciate my son Samuel's willingness to engage in this material and offer comments even as he and his girlfriend (now wife) asked the question, "Are we ready for the ring?"

I also appreciate our college pastor, Stefan Nitzschke, for engaging the material and encouraging some of our college students to test it. There are times when ideas sound a lot better in one's mind than they work in real life. It was very helpful to field-test the material.

This is now my third book-length project with New Growth Press. It is hard to believe that they still desire to work with me. I appreciate all their expertise to ensure that the product is as good as possible with my limitations and weaknesses.

Endnotes

1. Paul Tripp, *What Did You Expect? Redeeming the Realities of Marriage* (Crossway, 2012), updated edition titled *Marriage: 6 Gospel Commitments Every Couple Needs to Make* (Crossway, 2021).

2. Ernie Baker, *Marry Wisely, Marry Well* (Shepherd Press, 2016).

3. Milton Vincent, *The Gospel Primer for Christians* (Focus, 2008).

4. Dane Ortlund, *Gentle and Lowly: The Heart of Christ for Sinners and Sufferers* (Crossway, 2020).

5. Deepak Reju, *She's Got the Wrong Guy: Why Smart Women Settle* (New Growth Press, 2017).

6. A book could also be written entitled *He's Got the Wrong Girl*, warning men about the following women: (1) the adulteress, (2) the contentious one, (3) the free spender, (4) the gold digger, (5) the deceiver, etc.

7. Stephen Viars, *Putting Your Past in Its Place: Moving Forward in Freedom and Forgiveness* (Harvest House, 2011).

8. John Piper, *This Momentary Marriage: A Parable of Permanence* (Crossway, 2012).

9. Andrew David Naselli and J. D. Crowley, *Conscience: What It Is, How to Train It, and Loving Those Who Differ* (Crossway, 2016). You also might consider reading H. Wayne House, *Divorce and Remarriage: Four Christian Views* (IVP Academic, 1990), or Jim Newheiser, *Marriage, Divorce, and Remarriage: Critical Questions and Answers* (P&R Publishing, 2017).

10. Many have been helped by Dave Ramsey Financial Peace University, https://www.ramseysolutions.com/money/financial-peace. For a deeper theological evaluation but less practical help, see Craig Blomberg, *Neither Poverty Nor Riches: A Biblical Theology of Possessions*, New Studies in Biblical Theology, ed. D. A. Carson (IVP Academic, 2000).